'Y' OH 'Y'

(A SPEC-OP'S PROGRESS)

TONY NASH

Other works by Tony Nash:
The Mayhem in Norfolk thrillers:
Murder on Tiptoes
Murder by Proxy
Murder on the Back Burner
Murder on the Chess Board
Murder on the High 'C'
Bled and Breakfast

The John Hunter mysteries:
Carve Up
Single to Infinity
The Most Unkindest Cut
The Iago Factor
Blood Lines
Blockbuster
Beyond Another Curtain (Sequel to Blockbuster)
The Thursday Syndrome

The Harry Page thrillers:
Tripled Exposure
Unseemly Exposure

The Norfolk Farming Family Trilogy:
A Handful of Destiny
A Handful of Salt
A Handful of Courage

Hardrada's Hoard (with Richard Downing)
The Rarer Side of the Moon
Hell and High Water
The Devil Deals Death
The Makepeace Manifesto
The World's Worst Joke Book

*"Never mind; laugh it off; laugh it off; it's all part of life's rich pageant."*
(Arthur Marshall – *"The Games Mistress"* – 1937)

ACKNOWLEDGEMENT:
My sincere thanks to my good friend, Chris Boyd, who not only proof-read this book, but aided me with chronology and details that were somewhat dim in my memory.

LIST OF ABBREVIATIONS AND NICKNAMES
USED:
Sked – the schedule of working times used by a
station or network.
CO – Commanding Officer
SIGINT – Signals Intelligence
HUMINT – Human Intelligence
HA III – Hauptabteilung III – the Sigint Directorate
of the MIS
MIS also STASI – Ministerium für Staatsicherheit –
Ministry of State Security
SNCO – Senior Non-commissioned Officer
SHQ – Station Headquarters
SWO – Station Warrant Officer – usually in charge
of admin.
BZ – British Zone
RT – radio telephony – voice transmissions
MT – motor transport
Rupert – Army officer
Pongo – soldier
Retd. – retired
AMU – Air Force Maintenance Unit
Q – GCHQ
NAAFI – Navy, Army and Air Force Institute
QT – quiet
WO – Warrant Officer
Erk – an airman of very junior rank

CHAPTER ONE

It was not the most inspiring sight in the world.

Delhi in mid-monsoon season had nothing on RAF Compton Bassett as the ancient Swindon Omnibus Company 'Arab' bus, made by Guy Motors, wheezed to a stop close to the guardroom, its engine panting like an old, worn out dog trying to recover its breath after struggling to the top of the hill.

The contrast to my surroundings of the previous two years could not have been greater. A barely controlled despair attempted to overcome my usual 'half full' attitude to any adversity in life, and I had that gut-tightening 'What the hell have I done?' feeling we all know.

Those last two years I'd spent basking in the glorious sunshine of Southern Rhodesia, as it was called then, enjoying every minute of my Air Navigator training at RAF Gwelo, but after the swingeing cuts I was an intrepid birdman no longer.

Demobbed on Thursday, two weeks and four days earlier, on the third of April 1951, I had looked around at what Civvy Street offered and knew that whatever I opted for I would miss the 'Mob'.

For better or worse, it had got under my skin.

Mad? Sure - as a bloody hatter, but that was me. Being Taurus, every decision I've made in life has been almost instantaneous, and any regret shoved to one side.

Probably the most striking example of that decision making process came thirty-odd years after I left the RAF, when I sat in the hot seat of 'Who Wants To Be A Millionaire' and gabbled out an answer to the eight thousand pound question that I knew damned well to be wrong and actually knew the right answer, but then, with those five hundred watt floods and a camera lens rammed up against your eyes, it's easy for your mind to go completely ga-ga. That's my excuse, and I'm sticking with it.

In actual fact, both my wife and I were damned pleased I didn't win a huge sum, because in the week between my two appearances on the show we had dozens of phone calls and letters from people we vaguely knew, and a lot whom we didn't, with pleading requests – anything from "we can't afford shoes for our kids" to "you know we always liked you; could you help us out with our mortgage debts?"

Very few of them bothered to say 'Please'.

Two men turned up at our door during that week, one assuring me that he had been one of my bosom pals during my RAF days. I had never set eyes on him before.

The other was "a second cousin on my mother's side" who was researching the family history.

And, of course, every charity in the country was after me, at the door, by post and on the phone.

We were ex-directory, and the local newspaper snoops trawled the pubs in the area, asking if anyone knew our telephone number and address. One of the guys who worked for me, holding up the bar at his local, gave them both details, which they published, under the heading, *"LOCAL MAN GOES FOR THE MILLION"*.

I could have throttled him, but satisfied myself with a ten-minute, top of the voice blast, which seriously questioned, among other things, his parentage.

In point of fact, since I did not win the million, it made little difference.

The sad thing is that had I actually won that money we would have had to move.

The decision to rejoin made, a quick return visit to the local recruiting office in Norwich had me signed up as an erk headed for 'Air Signaller/Wireless Operator' training, with the admonition from the recruiting officer that any hopes I had of the former was pie in the sky, since after the cutbacks that trade was now just about a dead duck, and I had better resign myself to the latter.

Grabbing my kitbag as I rose to leave the bus and faced with a severe soaking, I forced the thought to the surface that at least I was still alive to be soaked, and that brought forth a wry grin as I thought back a couple of months.

The Hastings, which carried the number 624 and was to supposed to be flying us all the way back to Blighty, took off from Salisbury on time and the flight, though bumpy as usual from the late morning turbulence that preceded the afternoon 'duty cumulous', was pleasant enough and a nice contrast to the Avro Anson 19s I'd spent so many hours in. Flying always ceased at lunch time to avoid the three hundred foot, stomach wrenching plunges and uplifts of the post meridian, which preceded the evening thunderstorms, with their unbelievably fantastic displays of lightning, which went on till midnight on most evenings.

We landed at Nairobi in the late afternoon for an overnight stop and immediately decided to go into town to see the sights.

I made my first mistake on the bus, when, used to addressing all male coloureds as 'boy' – the standard appellation used in Rhodesia, I asked the bus driver as we were about to get off, 'What time does the bus collect here to go back to the airfield, boy?'

He jumped out of his seat, eyes alight with anger and flailing his arms in the air, 'I no boy! I bus driver! You no call me boy!'

He looked as if he was about to burst a blood vessel.

For an outburst like that in Rhodesia, he would have been yanked unceremoniously out of his bus, beaten severely about the head and carted straight off to jail.

It taught me an important lesson.

There was no apartheid in Kenya, and, of course, though we were ignorant of it, dissension was coming up to boiling point. It was only a scant twelve months later that the Mau Mau atrocities began, and I could easily envisage my bus driver clutching an AK47, shooting, torturing, beheading and disembowelling white settlers at the side of Dedan Kimathi, the Mau Mau leader. What a difference a few hundred miles made. The wave of uprising was rolling across Africa, and Rhodesia, although backward in that respect, would not be exempt.

The facilities provided at the airfield included a tiny cinema, and we trooped in, not knowing what to expect.

We might have known – it was *'Hellzapoppin',* with Ole Olson and Chick Johnson, which had been funny the first time we saw it at the Astra back at Gwelo. There was no plot to speak of, and the only bit which stuck in the memory was the delivery boy, carrying a small potted plant, who called gently and politely at the beginning of the film, '*Paging Mrs Jones, paging Mrs Jones*'' and reappeared at intervals throughout the entire film with an ever larger tree, becoming more and more desperate, until at the end he is in tears, driving a sixty-foot articulated lorry with an enormous fir tree and screaming, '*Mrs Jones*' at the top of his voice.

I doubt the film has aged well.

We walked along the banks of the wide, fast swirling river, also called the Nairobi, its waters the colour of strong tea, and I wondered idly how the fish managed to survive. If there were any, which I doubted, they would need to be able to feed by smell, because the visibility was zero.

Smell was what Nairobi was all about.

I was well used to animal odours, having been brought up on a farm, and helped my father with the two hundred pigs and other animals we had, but the incredible effluvia of Nairobi put the healthy smells of animals into the shade, and the pièce de résistance was the meat market, whose unbelievable pong almost knocked you off your feet.

Used to the cleanliness of an English butcher's shop, the sight of freshly slaughtered carcasses hanging in the strong sunlight and covered with what looked like a million bluebottles was unbelievable. How anyone eating any of that meat could survive constant and dangerous stomach upsets was just impossible to grasp, but the locals obviously did. The flies were having a field day, without being bothered in the least by those selling the meat. I guess they looked at the fly eggs as extra calories.

A few minutes was quite enough to spend there, but the smell of that market has stayed with me throughout my life, and I can still recall it now. The nearest thing to that miasma that I have come across was the German Stinkkäse that was once offered to me. How anyone ever managed to eat it I couldn't imagine – I certainly refused it, but at least it came in smaller quantities.

We spent the night in RAF transit accommodation at the aerodrome and took off the following morning, with the pilot making a detour, so that we could get a glimpse of Mount Kilimanjaro in the distance, before setting course for Aden.

The Hastings approached over the sea to touch down at RAF Khormaksar, whose well chosen station motto was *'Into The Remote Places'*, at tea time, and the skinny, ginger haired and moustachioed sergeant with his clipboard who assembled us as we de-planed said that there was not enough accommodation for all of us at Khormaksar and asked for three volunteers to go to alternative accommodation at 114 MU in Steamer Point for the night.

Ignoring the strict *'Never volunteer for anything'* admonition of my father, who had gone right through the First World War as a regular soldier, and managed to only get shot twice, I, Pete Green and Charlie Oldsworth, the 'three musketeers', always ready for a bit of skulduggery and with similar bizarre senses of humour, put our hands up, thinking we would be able to see a lot more of Aden than the others while we were there, and were told to go out of the building to the Jeep that was waiting for us and which would bring us back to the departure area at nine the next morning.

We enjoyed the ride, taking in the unusual sights and smells, blissfully unaware that we had been duped.

The driver of the Jeep dropped us off outside the mess and shrugged when I asked him if he would be picking us up on the morrow. It should have told me something.

In fact, after finally getting something to eat, having persuaded a disgruntled cook wanting to get off to his evening pleasures into fudging around to find us some leftovers, it was too late to leave camp and we sank a few bevvies in the NAAFI and crawled into bed.

At a quarter past eight, coming out of the cookhouse after breakfast the next morning, we heard an aircraft taking off and watched it with interest as it flew low above us.

Pete said it just before I did, 'Hey! That's our bloody Hastings!'

The '624' was plainly visible on its side.

No Jeep turned up for us, and after standing there sweating in the appalling heat for over half an hour we went in search of transport.

An unhelpful and uninterested SP in the guardroom listened to our story, shaking his head, and finally told us we would have to catch the bus.

That was an experience in itself, but with the help of an Indian bus driver who spoke some English, we eventually made it.

We were stopped by the guard and had to tell our tale again, then ran to the departure area, where we found our three kitbags standing in a forlorn little group in the middle of the floor, like a solitary stook of corn in a stubble field, forgotten by the harvesters.

There was no one in sight.

After standing around for over half an hour like an unwanted minority group we set off to look for SHQ and someone who could tell us what the hell was going on.

The SWO was not in his office, and his clerk had not a clue what we were talking about, but told us to wait while he made some enquiries and not to answer the phone.

He disappeared out of the door and was gone so long we began to wonder if he'd deserted, but eventually came back with an aged, overweight sergeant, his body tanned to dark leather and with a face so full of furrows that it seemed one could plant potatoes in it.

He looked us over with a lugubrious expression before asking, 'You are the three who volunteered to stay behind because the aircraft was overloaded, aren't you?'

Our combined, disbelieving, jabbering voices were stilled by his shout of 'Shut up!'

He asked for just one of us to speak and Pete told him our story, which made him nod knowingly.

'That's our beloved Sergeant Pettiford for you. Would you have volunteered if he'd told you the real reason?'

We looked at each other and shook our heads.

'Well,' he said, 'you're stuck with it now.' He seemed to derive pleasure from our discomfort.

I asked, 'When can we expect the next aircraft?'

He shrugged, 'Your guess is as good as mine; a week, a month. That's if you're lucky; could be three.'

Charlie asked the all-important question, 'Can we get some pay?'

The sergeant nodded, 'I guess I can organise that for you.'

'And is it okay to go out of camp?'

'Of course, but watch the locals. They'll have the shirts off your backs before you can say 'Shufti cush', and on that subject for Christ's sake don't touch the local whores or you'll regret it for the rest of your lives. They're poxed up to the eyebrows.'

He did not warn us about the one thing which we needed most to be warned about, but then he probably didn't realise he was dealing with three idiots.

He was as good as his word, and a hour or so later we wandered out past the guardroom with local currency in our pockets, the East African shilling, then at par with the English shilling, which made bargaining easy for us.

One of the other erks had told us that the Crater was worth a visit, and where to catch the bus.

It was an experience, with sights and smells unlike any we'd seen before. It was a unique place, where the average daily temperature was over a hundred Fahrenheit and the rainfall less than two inches a year.

The novelty soon palled, and we caught another bus back and down to Steamer Point.

The harbour and beaches were crowded, and we wandered along observing everything. There were several vessels at anchor, quite a distance away across the bay. One of the most distant, at about a mile and a half, was an American destroyer.

Suddenly, Pete flung his arm out, pointing to the beach below us, 'Look! Canoes we can hire. Let's paddle out to that Yankee ship and shout "Daddy" at the sailors.'

I had spent many hours a week on the water during most of my life before joining up, either in my one-man canoe on the river behind our house or punt-gunning after waterfowl, and was game for anything of that sort, but the craft he was pointing at were vastly different from anything I had ever sailed in before.

To call them 'canoes' needed a great stretch of the imagination.

They were literally nothing but rough-hewn, hollowed out tree trunks, sharpened at both ends into something resembling a prow and a stern; the most ungainly vessels imaginable, but they obviously floated. The paddles were unwieldy straight branches, flattened at one end.

We began the haggling process with the native owner, a wizened, dried up old man, wearing nothing but a loin cloth, who spoke only Arabic, of which at that time I had no knowledge at all, but money spoke, and he took several of our notes with a shrug after I had with a circling finger described an hour on my watch, but kept urgently trying to tell us something. We should have found an interpreter.

Pete and I began to shove the two-seater towards the water and Charlie struggled with the single-seater, shouting for us to help him launch.

We finally had both ungainly vessels floating and climbed in.

They were dreadful beasts to try and move, but we made some slow progress.

After twenty minutes I had had enough; it was tiring, with little reward for effort, and the American vessel still looked the same distance away.

'Let's go back, Pete.' I suggested, and he agreed.

He shouted over to Charlie and we turned the dugouts in a huge circle and pointed them back towards the beach.

A few minutes later, with the soporific splash of the paddles and the debilitating heat almost lulling me to sleep, I dabbed the paddle towards the water again – and hit something solid!

I'd been looking ahead, but swung my head round to see what I'd hit, expecting anything but what I saw: a dark grey body that looked the size of a nuclear submarine only inches away from the canoe, and with a huge triangular fin in the middle.

At that moment the enormous body plunged beneath the waves, leaving a bloody great hole in the water. The laws of physics regarding the displacement of water being what they are, that hole was filled mighty fast, and the canoe tipped dangerously, itself trying to do some of that filling up, while I swung my body as hard as I could to the left to counterbalance the movement.

Pete swung round angrily, 'What the fuck are you doing!'

I tried to shout 'Shark!' but no sound came out of my mouth, not even a hiss. Shock had lost me my voice.

His anger mounted, 'What? Stop pissing about!'

I tried again, mouthing the word over and over again, but he didn't get it and continued swearing about me trying to tip us over.

At that moment the shark tried again, its huge body rising higher than our gunwale, the top of its dorsal fin level with my eyes.

Pete's mouth dropped open, and his eyes went wide.

The canoe rolled again, but this time both of us leant the other way.

He turned and began to paddle as if the Devil himself was at his back. I did the same and we tried out damndest to get that chunk of wood up on a first-degree plane, with no success whatsoever.

Charlie had been several yards in front, paddling with ease, but we passed him, doing at least a quarter of a knot faster the way we were paddling, and as we drew level we both pointed at the water and tried to shout 'Shark!'.

Though it was not the moment for merriment, I noticed that Pete too had lost the use of his voice.

Charlie, in his turn, went through the 'What?' routine and kept shaking his head, not understanding what we were trying to tell him.

Then the shark did another repeat performance and he saw it.

This time we saw its whole body. It was more than twice as long as our canoe.

The beach seemed miles away, but we sweated buckets as we tried to reach it.

The shark did its thing every couple of minutes all the way in, and it was only by sheer luck that our counterbalancing kept us afloat and in the canoe.

Charlie was lucky. He escaped entirely the shark's attentions.

At last the beach neared and we saw scores of dark faces eagerly watching the display, obviously hoping it would become a blood sport.

The last attack was only forty yards or so from the shore, and I guess the shark realised it would ground itself if it went in any closer.

The sound of the sand grinding on the bow was the finest I had ever heard in my life, but neither of us was about to step out of the canoe with that beast so close by.

Many willing hands dragged us up the beach, and then we almost fell out onto the blessed sand, worn out.

Charlie arrived and was pulled up too.

The little native who owned the canoes was doing a song and dance around us, gesticulating madly and repeating over and over words similar to those he had used before we launched. Too late, I realised he had been trying to warn us not to go out too far.

Though I had forgotten about it, I'd read somewhere that the shark population of the Red Sea is one of the highest per square mile of all the seas in the world, with over forty species roaming around in it.

During a long and adventurous life I have been 23 times within an inch, and sometimes a couple of millimetres, of death, but I have never again been so utterly terrified as I was that day, with the atavistic fear of my flesh being ripped apart by the teeth of that leviathan.

We learnt a few days later from an English resident that we were not alone in having attracted that shark's attention. There had been more than a few deaths among the fishermen who used such craft. The clever creatures had apparently learnt that method of turning over canoes and did it with great effect.

The Aden shark problem was put into stark relief six weeks later.

Part of the sea was fenced off with heavy steel netting near the base for use by the British forces and their families.

Called the Lido, it was used every day by scores of men, women and children.

The Station Commander's wife was one of those bathing one fateful day, when a shark located a small hole in the steel netting and forced its body through.

It was sheer fate that the CO's wife was its target. It took off her leg and killed her.

There, but for the grace of God…

Life in Aden, with nothing to do, became boring, and most days, after roaming around Steamer Point or the Crater, we spent playing three-card brag in the hut.

We tried the cinema, not in the least surprised to find that the film showing was *'Hellzapoppin'*! That was the movie for a month. At last, a different one was shown: *'It Came From Another World'.* The film was so dire that we decided the creature would have been a damned sight better if it had stayed there. Following that we had the delights of *'Ace in the Hole'*, featuring Kirk Douglas and Jan Sterling. They showed only the best at the Astra! It seemed from the advance programme that *'Horatio Hornblower'* would be shown, but we were long gone if that ever happened.

It was the year that *'The African Queen'* came out, but it was years later before I had the chance to view it.

All good things come to an end, they say, and at last a scruffy looking erk was sent to find us, with the information that we would be leaving the next morning.

Promptly at eight we reported to the departure area and outside the window saw an ancient Avro Anson, looking as if it had been sand-blasted. Even the RAF roundels were tatty.

Take off was supposed to be at eight-thirty, but it was ten past nine when two relatively ancient airmen strolled in as if they had all the time in the world, a flight sergeant pilot with a well stocked beer belly bulging over his shorts and a phenomenal Jimmy Edwards moustache, and a sergeant navigator whose skeletal frame and jerky movements made him appear like a puppet being operated by some unseen puppet master with invisible strings.

What impressed us most were the two and a half rows of medal ribbons on the breast of the pilot's tunic and a similar amount on that of the navigator.

They included all the war medals and the pilot wore the DFM and bar. The Distinguished Flying Medal was not something handed out with the laundry and demanded a great deal of respect.

We learnt from one of the cooks at the next stop that they had both joined up at the start of the war and each had thousands of hours in their flying log books. The pilot, the cook told us, had flown just about everything in the book and had earned one of his DFMs flying a Mosquito.

They nodded a greeting and the pilot jerked his head towards the Anson.

We moseyed out in front of them and climbed in through the door after the dispatcher opened it for us.

After a walk-round external check, the two aircrew boarded the plane and went to their respective seats.

Not a word had been exchanged between them, nor was it as they went through the pre-flight checks.

The engines were started, the Anson was taxied out and we were in the air, headed we knew not where.

After the first hour the only thing beneath us was sand - sand stretching to the horizon on both sides of the aircraft. We seemed to be flying at about eight thousand feet and the temperature was comfortable, though down below it was way over a hundred in the shade, and there was none.

The kite flew on monotonously and we stupidly remarked several times that at least the wings were flapping. Those who knew the Anson well had warned us that if they were not flapping it was time to strap on the parachutes.

After seven hours of that we felt the nose go down, and Jimmy Edwards landed at some tiny speck of nothing and taxied up to a refuelling bowser, where the tanks were topped up.

Our stomachs were grumbling, and thirst was becoming a problem. Any hope of refreshments from this hell hole seemed to be out of the question, but the navigator surprised us. He unfolded his awkward frame from his seat, picked up a closed box we hadn't noticed before and brought it down to us.

He placed it on the floor between us and waved his hand to indicate that we should dig in.

Pete removed the lid and we found piles of sandwiches, bananas, oranges and apples, along with half a dozen cans of soft drink.

Looking forward I noticed that the pilot and nav were also munching and guzzling. They had their show off pat after years of working together.

Their chow finished, and with the bowser disconnected and the tanks closed, the two up front exchanged seats, and with the navigator driving we took to the air again. It was not according to the book, but these two had obviously done it many times before.

Another six hours of sand saw the nose dip again, and yet another bleak spot in the desert welcomed our arrival. The navigator's landing was just as smooth as that of the pilot.

Jimmy Edwards got out of his seat when his companion braked to a halt outside what seemed to be the sole building and came back to where we sat.

He spoke for the first time, 'Hope you enjoyed the bus ride, lads. Sorry we can't take you the rest of the way. We're heading back to Aden after we load up.'

He disappointed me. He didn't sound anything like Jimmy Edwards.

I asked him, 'Where are we?'

He smiled grimly, 'The arse end of beyond – Wadi Haifa, on what the locals call the shit-laden Sweet Water Canal. Enjoy it.'

A corporal, with sweat staining the sand that was plastered on his face, stood by the plane with a clipboard when we descended.

He checked our names and then mumbled, 'Hut three, follow me.'

There were other buildings, but not many of them, and they were the same colour as the sand. And that was all there was at Wadi Haifa – sand, sand and more sand, and it was in the air with the stiff wind, quickly getting into our hair, eyes and noses.

The temperature must have been over the ton, and carrying our kitbags we quickly became sweat soaked, following the corporal as he plodded towards a hut.

It was a relief to get inside out of the sand, but the heat was almost unbearable.

The hut was laid out with ten beds, four of them made up, with personal items on the bedside lockers, the rest with blankets folded on them.

Pete asked him, 'When do we get out of here?'

He shrugged, 'Buggered if I know, mate.'

'Is there anyone we can ask?'

He laughed, 'Sure. You can ask anyone, but they won't know either. You'll go when the next crate with seats available that's going in your direction drops in.'

'Is there anything to do here?'

'No, except we do have a film on Thursdays. Jock Gray has a 16mm projector.'

Groaning inside I asked, 'What's the film?'

I knew I should not have bothered, 'It's a comedy.' He scratched his head, 'Can't remember what it's called.'

'Not '*Hellzapoppin*' by any chance?'

His face brightened, 'Ar! That's it. Bloody good. Seen it twice already.'

He was way behind us on that score.

'Where do we eat?'

'The mess is three down, that way.'

'No NAAFI?'

'You must be joking, mate. Where do you think this is?'

We were there for six days, bored out of our skulls, just eating, drinking and trying to relax in the heat. We got to know the four airmen sharing our accommodation, and they agreed it was probably the worst posting in the world, but it was a good place to save money - there was nothing to spend it on.

Finally, a Hastings landed and the same corporal who had met us at the Anson came and told us to 'Get your things together quickly. You're taking off in ten minutes.'

We had to scramble, but just made it.

This time we were told our destination: RAF Ismailia, in the Canal Zone. The aircraft was not going back to the UK.

Ismailia was much more organised than our previous stops, and was a largish affair, mainly tented, but with a highly organised Station Headquarters, and our arrival was, amazingly, expected.

We were again met at the aircraft and taken to the tent in which we would spend the next five weeks. Lounging on their cots were four members of the RAF Regiment, the first time we had come into contact with 'rock apes', as they were generally referred to by RAF personnel. They greeted us civilly enough and seemed like normal human beings, with the same gripes as everyone else. One was a big Geordie lad who jumped up and shook hands.

The erk who had conveyed us to the tent told us that as 'supernumaries' we would be required to carry out certain duties during our stay there, and that we should report to the SWOs office the next morning at eight.

On the way to the mess hall for tea, we passed the Astra cinema and looked at the coming attractions and present bill.

It was no surprise to see that '*Hellzapoppin*' had star billing that week.

After a couple of beers in the NAAFI, I settled down under canvas for the first time since my Boy Scout days. The cots were uncomfortable, and even with just a sheet over me I was too hot, but eventually drifted off to sleep.

In my dream there were explosions, and I suddenly sat bolt upright – they were real.

All three of us had woken, but the four 'rock apes' were sound asleep.

There were more explosions, which I now recognised as rifle shots, and I shook Geordie awake.

He'd had a few more bevvies than we had and groaned, 'Wassup?'

'There's shooting!' I blurted.

'Oh, is there?' He sounded completely uninterested and turned as if to go back to sleep.

'What is it? Who's doing the shooting?'

'Oh, don't worry; it's only the bloody Ay-rabs.'

'Who are they shooting at?' I couldn't understand; we weren't at war with them.

'They shoot some of the arc lights out every night for fun. Go back to sleep.'

We found out the next day that the camp residents generally called it the 'Evening Chorus', and that it was a regular feature of camp life. Any smashed bulbs were replaced each morning.

We were to be issued with rifles ourselves just a few hours later, when we presented ourselves at SHQ, where half a dozen three-and-a-half-ton lorries were standing, their engines running, and with drivers standing beside them.

A sergeant armourer asked us several searching questions, to ensure that we were acquainted with firearms and their safety, and then issued each of us and three other airmen with a Lee-Enfield .303 rifle and nine rounds of ammunition.

'You're on escort duty while you're here. You'll be shot at, but if you shoot back, even one round, you'll be facing a Court of Inquiry, so don't be tempted. They're bloody terrible shots and the rifles they use are mostly about a hundred years old. Couldn't hit a barn door at ten paces. And you'll never see them. They just melt into the sand dunes.'

Pete asked, 'Has anyone ever been shot?'

The sergeant laughed, 'Have a look at the gharries.' He pointed to the one nearest us, which had a dent in one of the doors and a hole in the wooden side of the body half way along. 'That's about as near as they ever get.'

Pete made his eyes go like saucers, 'Too bloody close for me. Aaaahh!'

We fell about laughing, although it was no joking matter.

The trucks were headed for Port Said at the top of the Canal, to pick up supplies from the docks, a distance of forty-five miles, and we installed ourselves on the passenger seats, rifles in between our knees. I did not load the rifle, but kept the bullets in my pocket. No way did I want a Court of Inquiry, and for some reason I believed the sergeant.

The driver held out his hand and muttered, 'Jim Casey'. From the accent I didn't need to ask where he hailed from. Every syllable had Belfast stamped all over it.

We were second in line, and with the usual Bedford grinding of gears in the 'crash box' we set off.

The journey was slightly more interesting topographically than the flight, since at least there were Arab dhows and other shipping to be seen on the Canal.

I saw no shooters and heard nothing, even with the window opened, partly to keep the smoke out of the cab, since both Jim Casey and I were chain smokers, and was surprised to learn when we reached our destination that the fifth truck in the little convoy had acquired another bullet hole in the bodywork.

It was interesting enough, watching the trucks being loaded by the native workers, and some enterprising lad had arranged refreshments for us.

Loaded up, we reversed our course and arrived back at Ismailia in time for lunch.

Afterwards, we headed back to the tent, which was empty.

And empty of all of my and Pete's possessions, even our spare underwear and socks.

Thinking that our accommodation had been changed while we were away, and our things moved ready for us, we didn't worry, but lounged around on our cots, relaxing after the terribly tough morning we had endured.

Geordie pushed his way through the entrance flap half an hour later, and I asked why we were being moved.

He looked puzzled until I pointed out that none of our possessions was in the tent.

The look on his face told us a different story and he swore continuously and with great inventiveness for almost a minute straight, mentioning the name of one of the other 'rock apes' several times.

'He's a clifty wallah, Tony', he said, 'Got his 'Ds' for that.'

I was puzzled, 'What's a clifty wallah and what are his 'Ds', Geordie?'

'He's a thief; can't help it, and he was given a dishonourable discharge. Did six months in the glasshouse before being put on the plane home. Don't worry, I'll get your things back.'

He disappeared and came back, holding a hollering fellow 'rock ape' by a twisted ear.

The interrogation that followed would in no way have been sanctioned by the legal system of any western country, and we winced as 'R' took his severe punishment, at first vehemently denying any knowledge of the thefts, but Geordie went even further, making me believe that 'R' would never father any children, and at last he admitted that he had taken our things. Further battering elucidated that he had buried them in the sand outside the camp, but could not remember where.

Geordie, breathing heavily from his exertions, looked at us and shook his head, 'Sorry.'

We spent days looking, but never found anything. We were left with what we stood up in. The presents I had bought for the family were gone too.

The strange thing was that I felt really sorry for the badly beaten thief, realising too late that he was not quite right in the head, something that had not been obvious before, though Geordie must have known it.

The mixture went on as before for the seven weeks we were stuck in Ismailia, doing the Port Said run every weekday and sometimes on Sundays. At least, it got us out of parades. Three times the lorry I was in was hit, twice far back near the tail, but one shot smashed the side window, and I was hit with a tiny fragment of glass, which sliced a small piece of skin out of my forehead, making me, I believe, the only casualty of the whole period, though it was only the start of something much bigger. The Egyptian Revolution of July in the following year led to open aggression against the British and French, and then there were some real casualties.

We found the culprit on the floor of the lorry – a flattened piece of lead. They were using ball shot, and I guessed they had to be firing antique muzzle loaders.

At last, when we had almost given up hope, a Hastings headed for England landed and we were told we were to be passengers on it.

Imagine our chagrin when we saw its tail number: 624!

A relatively short flight saw us landing at RAF Luqa, in Malta, and the overnight stay allowed us to revisit that evening the notorious Straight Street, known not too affectionately to every serviceman who had ever visited Malta as 'The Gut'. As the name suggests, the street is straight and sloping. Friends who have visited Malta recently and been to the area have told me that it is now perfectly respectable, but at the time of which I am writing it put anything modern Amsterdam can do far into the shade. Literally anything went. Though badgered insistently to indulge in the most dubious of female and other delights every few yards, including a show which involved a donkey, we, thank God, were savvy enough to refuse them. We did drink at a number of the establishments as we wandered the length of the 'Gut', however, and watched the entertainment, and were not in the least surprised when we looked through the open door of one bar to see a British serviceman in khaki uniform, his shorts down around his ankles, fornicating frantically with a whore up against the front of the bar, with everyone in the place shouting boozy encouragement.

Oh, yes, anything went. Autre pays, autres moeurs.

Nicely inebriated, we were in another bar in a better part of town when we were approached by a florid looking, middle-aged gentleman dressed in an immaculate white suit, who had got up from a table at the back, where he had been sitting on his own.

He introduced himself as Major Strickland, a name that meant nothing to any of us, and told us that his family more or less ruled Malta. He himself, he told us, had been Prime Minister at one time.

Oh, yeah, we thought, and exchanged knowing glances, but we were polite to him and even more polite when another round of drinks appeared on the table, and he made a motion with his hand to indicate that the barman should put them on his tab.

Memory becomes dim at this stage, relative to the amount of other drinks that followed, but after about an hour he suggested we decamp to the Royal Malta Yacht Club, of which, he said, he was President; another likely story!

Somehow we found ourselves in a luxurious, chauffeur-driven, late model white Rolls Royce and shortly afterwards arrived at the Yacht Club, which was clearly a popular meeting place for its members, and was almost full.

The disbelieving and downright angry looks we received as every eye in the place turned towards us when we staggered through the door of that elite club behind our host I still remember now – three already well-oiled RAF lads in less than pristine khaki shorts and shirts definitely had no place among that austere, high society crowd, but our host, if aware of the hostility, blithely ignored it. He was greeted by the head waiter with obvious deference, and we were shown to a table, where more drinks appeared as if by magic. The novelty soon seemed to wear off; the patrons went back to their conversations, and we were ignored.

The man who called himself Major Strickland plied us into the early hours with as much as we wanted to drink, and we certainly took advantage of the opportunity.

Sometime around two in the morning found us back in the Rolls and travelling back to Luqa, accompanied by the 'Major', himself several sheets in the wind, but still the perfect gentleman.

We poured ourselves out of the vehicle at the guardroom, said almost tearful 'Cheerios' and staggered into camp.

It was some years before I came across an article in a magazine referring to a Major Strickland of Malta and was amazed to read that there had indeed been such a gentleman, who had been Prime Minister of the Island – Lord Gerald Strickland, Count della Catana, and for a moment wondered if the man we met could have been real after all, but then I read a bit further and found that Lord Strickland had died in August 1940 and had sired no sons.

It remains a mystery who our benefactor was that evening, but two things are certain: he was extremely well off and if he was not the actual President he was clearly an important member of the Royal Malta Yacht Club.

We landed at Lyneham, in Wiltshire, late in the afternoon, and were whisked off to some accommodation at RAF Clyffe Pypard, a strange little station which had once been operational, with a 1500 yard grass runway, but was now relegated to being an accommodation centre for Lyneham.

There was nothing to do after tea but go to see the film being shown by one of the erks on a sixteen mil projector.

The name of the film? You'd never guess in a thousand years!

CHAPTER TWO

So, after two days at 5 Personnel Disposal Unit, Hednesford, the first place I had been sent to after re-joining the RAF, here I was, back in Wiltshire, at the gates of Compton Bassett.

I pulled up the collar of my greatcoat and waded through the inch of water flooding the road outside the guardroom, booked in and was told to go to the SWO's office, where I received the dreaded 'blue chit', which had to be signed by everyone including God before one was officially 'on the strength', and was told by the corporal who had given me the chit to report to Hut 19, 'Y' lines. He showed me where it was on the map pinned to the wall.

It was the first time I had been associated with something designated 'Y'.

I had no idea that the association was to last throughout the next twenty years.

It was a long walk through the deserted and desolate lines of huts, and I was well and truly drenched by the time I pushed the outer door of the hut open.

Just inside, I found the ubiquitous pile of foot pads that I thought I'd seen the last of, and realised that Compton must be a bullshit camp. We had used them all the time in Rhodesia, trying to keep the lino on the floor of the hut shining so highly that one could clearly see one's reflexion in it, buffing it up with our feet to back up the long-handled push-pull polishing blocks that were used every evening.

I pulled a couple of them out, placed my feet on them and pushed open the inner door.

I then stopped open-mouthed at the sight that greeted me.

The hut was empty, except for one person.

That one person was six feet three tall, built like the proverbial brick outhouse, and black as the ace of spades – the blackest black man I had ever seen.

As my knowledge of black people, give or take the bus driver in Nairobi, had been overlaid with threats of the Apartheid Laws, I had no idea how to proceed.

Did this apparition speak English? How should I address him?

Speaking very clearly and distinctly, in case he had difficulty understanding, I asked, 'Which beds are free?'

I heard, though did not comprehend, a string of highly accented language: 'Achweelmonyeveachoiceyekenyecanputeyerheedd uneonywhereupyonend'.

I'd learnt some Swahili and Mashona, but it sounded nothing like either of those. I luckily did not do a Crocodile Dundee and ask, 'What tribe are you?', though something like it did cross my mind, I must admit.

In fact, the accent, though much harsher, was like that of two of my friends in Rhodesia, Sandy Mackintosh, a terrific piano player with whom I had served, and Don Maclennon, who had offered to buy me out of the RAF and give me a job in his electronics company, leading to an early directorship, with the admonition, 'But I advise you that you ought perhaps not to take up the offer, because one day, and it may not be this year, next year, or even this decade, but in this country there will one day be a bloodbath, black against white.' How right he was.

But back to Hut 19: I blurted, 'I beg your pardon?'

The apparition, whose name I learnt was Jackie Ray, and with whom I became fast friends, grinned, showing a mouthful of pearly white teeth, and repeated his information at about a fifth of the speed: 'Ach, weel, mon, ye've a choice, ye ken. Ye can pute yer heed dune onywhere up yon end.'

I shook my head, 'Where on earth do you come from?'

The grin widened, 'Ah was born and bred in the Gorbals, mon.'

I quickly learnt that Jackie was a boxer and a good one. Born black in the Gorbals, he'd had to learn to fight at a very early age to survive, and he'd come out on top. It took several weeks before I could instantly translate every word he said, but eventually found it easy. Before we left Compton I had watched him fight four times, and he won every bout easily.

There were a few Caribbean men in the Air Force, but Jackie was the only black man I ever came across during my time in the Mob.

I remember him with affection. I don't know if he is still alive, but I have made him immortal in my '*Mayhem in Norfolk*' murder mysteries, in the guise of Detective Sergeant John Bell, who appears first of all in *"Murder on Tiptoes"* and is one of the team of detectives in all seven books in that series.

Bell is something of a composite character, since I have also put into his mouth the phrase, '*Ach, ma grannie's arse*', used so often by another friend of mine - Warrant Officer 'Jock' Dempster, who sadly, like so many of my earlier colleagues, has gone to meet the Chief Operator in the sky.

Jackie was alone in the hut, and I wondered why. He told me that it was sports afternoon, and he had permission to miss the activity because he was boxing that evening.

The rain had eased to a steady downpour, and I set off to get the required signatures on the 'blue chit', wondering how many of them I could get away with signing myself, a trick I had learnt from another old airman.

Hating dentists and being scared of them ever since the age of eleven, after hearing my brother screaming blue murder while in the chair when we went for a school check-up, at which time I had taken to my heels and didn't go back, I always signed that one, along with several of the others I thought I could get away with, and the ruse was undetected for seventeen years, until on one posting the dentist just happened to be conversing with the doctor when I went for the latter's signature and told me he might as well have a look at me right away, since he was about to go back to his surgery.

He hit the roof when he looked in my mouth. 'How long ago did you see a dentist?' was the demand, and I admitted. 'Seventeen years, sir.'

'You've been signing your own chit, haven't you?'

I had to admit I had.

'Your mouth is a bloody mess!' he almost yelled. 'How long have you got before you leave?'

'Day after tomorrow, sir.' I told him.

'Bloody hell!' he complained, 'We'll never do it in time. Stay in that chair.'

An hour and a half later he stood back, satisfied, 'Well, it wasn't as bad as I thought after all. Just five fillings. Don't ever forge the dentist's signature on your chit again, you hear me? The health of your teeth controls the health of your entire body.'

Despite his admonition I did continue to sign my own chit, for the rest of my entire service, but he had done something important for me: I was no longer afraid of dentists. He had been very gentle, and I hadn't felt a thing.

During the rest of that first day at Compton, other new trainees arrived in dribs and drabs, and we introduced ourselves to each other.

Strangely, after leaving there, I never saw any of them again.

Around four o'clock the lads who had been playing sports returned boisterously, their PT kit soaked.

More introductions.

Being old hands, having been on the camp at least three days, they told me what I needed to know to get around.

I was intrigued to learn from a rotund, ginger haired Welsh lad, whose face was a mass of freckles and who called himself Dafydd, that the tea in the mess was to be avoided at all costs.

'Laced with bromide, it is. Bugger up your sex life, it will.' Years later, I remembered his strange syntax when I saw the film 'Star Wars', and listened to that delightful little character Yoda speaking. The accent wasn't that different either.

Since my sex life at that time was non-existent I didn't see how bromide in the tea mattered, but I had never served with women before, and at Compton Bassett there was a fair sprinkling of WAAFs. The raging testosterone of the young men around them ensured that they would become the objects of much chasing, and I would be in the forefront of the assault, with a singular lack of success.

There was general laughter at the Welsh lad's words, and one of the others asked, 'Who have you been banging then, Dafydd? That girl with the horn-rimmed specs you were trying to chat up in the NAAFI this morning?'

Dafydd blushed to the roots of his hair. 'I only offered to buy her a cup of tea.'

'So that she would let you into her drawers.'

He blushed some more. Like many of the lads in that hut, he was still a virgin.

We were classed up, seventeen lads and three women, two of them young – a plain and pleasant brunette called Kathy and a statuesque blonde, Elizabeth – the most beautiful girl I had ever laid eyes on up to that date, and icy with it, and the other what we thought of as an old woman, since her hair had turned prematurely grey. She was, in fact, only twenty-seven – Grace, a charming woman I got to know well by the end of the course, and wise beyond her years.

From well before she left school until a few months before joining the WAAF, she had devoted herself to nursing her sick mother.

When her mother passed away, she was stunned to learn that the house she lived in, which she had always understood was owned by her mother, was not. It was merely rented, and she was given one month's notice to quit. Not knowing what to do, and with no money, the RAF seemed to be the only possible solution. Notwithstanding those circumstances, she applied herself diligently to the course and came out close to the top.

She and I became good friends, without the least thought of hanky-panky. I think with me she felt safe, and we talked of many things, including personal relationships. She was very down to earth and gave me good advice on how one should treat women, although I had the impression she had never had a relationship with a man. When we broached the subject, she said she did not want one. She did let slip once that her father had badly ill-treated her mother before going off with a younger woman. Looking back and remembering some of the things she said and inferred, I believe that he had sexually abused Grace and left her with permanent psychological scars. At that time, things like that were never talked about. It would have explained her 'hands-off' approach with men.

Even at my relatively young age at the time I recognised a woman who would have made someone a wonderful, no nonsense wife, and I hope she did meet and marry someone eventually. Strangely enough, by the end of the course I believe I was a little in love with her. I have never forgotten her, at least.

Like all my peers, I spent many fruitless hours attempting to chat up Kathy, Elizabeth and the WAAFs in other classes.

It was only towards the end of the course that we found out that the Ice Maiden, Elizabeth, had been handing it out every night to one of the married corporal instructors, almost from day one. He was, in my view, a really ugly bugger; a weedy individual with pockmarked, jaundiced skin and a drooping moustache, but he had a car – and those two stripes.

The only one of us who was getting more than his fair share of feminine delights was Jim, who had the bed next to mine. A down-to-earth, worldly wise Cockney, he had found a WAAF whose libido matched his own, which was something several clicks north of a jack rabbit in the Spring. For the sake of protecting the not so innocent, I'll call her Jane.

Each night he would stagger back into his bed, often well after lights out, complaining about how she had stripped his thread.

This went on for several weeks, until one evening when he said he felt like giving it a miss and asked me if I wanted to 'take her on'.

'Tell her I've been put on jankers. She wants to go to the dance and then she'll want to screw. She knows the places.'

I needed no second bidding. She was no beauty; only five feet five and dumpy, with a little pot belly, but I was ready to sail into any port in a storm.

She just shrugged when I said Jim was on jankers, took my arm and headed for the gate and the Thursday hop in Calne Town Hall.

We danced every number, and I found out that she was a smart little mover, a delight to dance with, and I ought to know: for the three years before I joined the RAF I had danced four nights a week at the Samson and Hercules Ballroom in Norwich, and the other two weekday evenings I spent at the Norman School of Dancing, on All Saints Green. I was a dancing fool, a genuine '*Man, when he goes, he's Twinkletoes*' type – mad keen. Her only fault was that while she danced her mind was obviously on sex, which she made quite clear by the way she rubbed her body against mine so blatantly that it had the usual effect, and made me wonder if we would be kicked out by the management. But hell, I was enjoying it so much I didn't care.

At quarter past nine, she suggested fish and chips, and we left the hall and bought cod and chips twice at the chippie just down the road and scoffed them on the spot.

She licked her fingers and suggested, 'Shall we find somewhere?'

I told her to 'lead on', and she grinned and did so, her hand holding mine.

She knew the spots all right, but so did others, and after we'd been into three dark alleys where couples were already engaged in various stages of coitus she stood under a street lamp looking doubtful and a bit peeved.

I asked, 'Is there nowhere else?'

She shrugged, and we began to look.

The only place we could find that was dark was a small concrete pool, with forty-five degree sloping grass banks, about eight feet from the top to the water below.

It looked dodgy, but there was nowhere else.

Knickers, cotton, blue, WAAFs for the use of were removed without any prompting from me and placed in a pocket, and she lay down at the top of the slope.

I followed, ready for action, but each time we moved even a trifle one of us slipped, either a few inches or a foot or more.

When my foot went into the water we scrambled back up to the top and tried again….and again….and again.

After the fifth attempt, and with two wet feet, the craziness of the situation got to me and I started to giggle.

It was contagious, and in a very short time we were both howling with laughter as we clawed our way to the top and over it.

Knickers, cotton, blue, WAAFs for the use of were pulled back on, and arm in arm we ambled off to catch the bus back to camp.

Some years later I was to discover that the knickers issued to WAAF officers were white, and, if not exactly silk, were of a much finer material. But then, that is another story.

We had one parting kiss at the WAAF lines and parted chums.

Jim was lying on his bed when I returned to the hut and lifted his eyebrows in query.

I shook my head and he asked, 'Why?'

I told him, 'Long story. Ask her.'

He had a funny look on his face, which at the time I didn't understand. It looked strangely like disappointment.

Six weeks later 'Jane' was no longer stationed at Compton. She had been discharged – pregnant. That little pot belly had grown somewhat.

I can't prove it, but I now believe that she had very recently learnt that she was pregnant, and when she had confided that fact to Jim, the two of them had cooked up a scheme to find a father for the foetus that would let him off the hook. She would have lied about the date of impregnation and lined me up for a shotgun wedding. Naïve as I was at that time, I would probably have believed her, and it would have been too late when I found out I had been had.

Good old Newton saved the day. Thanks to the laws of gravitation, perhaps aided by that little pot belly I'd had a lucky escape.

Work-wise, the course went well, and particularly for me, since I had earned my Signaller's Badge in the Boy Scouts, reaching a Morse speed of 12 words per minute and a Semaphore speed, if I remember correctly, of 6 words per minute, so the early teaching – dit-dah is 'A', dah-dit-dit-dit is 'B' variety - had me yawning.

The scouts used the same measurement of a 'word' as the Services: five letters or figures, meaning that twelve words a minute indicated that one was reading or sending 60 characters in sixty seconds, one per second, which sounds a lot, but in fact is not.

My Morse reception speed gradually increased to twenty wpm and stuck there for a couple of weeks before rapidly improving to twenty-fives after I had practised day after day with nothing but mixed figure and letter groups, deliberately including in many groups the hardest letters like 'Z' and 'X', which appear rarely in ordinary text. Reception speed is also affected by an operator's automatic expectation of the next letter in a word, which comes with practice, and with the groups I was using there was no such expectation. When I went back to plain language I was so much faster.

For some reason I have never been able to understand, we spent many hours learning about radio theory and the inner workings of receivers. It was pretty crazy, since everyone in the radio trades knows perfectly well that when a set goes wrong, the incontrovertible advice from On High regarding its rehabilitation applies: *The operator knows you've got to kick it, and the mechanic knows where you've got to kick it, but the technician knows how hard you've got to kick it.*

There was no way we operators were ever going to be allowed to repair a piece of wireless equipment, though most of us have kicked one at some time. I certainly have!

We did end up with the knowledge that putting one's hand inside a receiver connected to the mains was not a particularly clever idea, unless one had suicide in mind, and some of the teaching must have stuck, because to this day I can remember that a superheterodyne receiver mixes the incoming signal with the output of an unmodulated VFO – a variable frequency oscillator, so that the output is a fixed frequency that is the difference between the other two. I don't know how I could possibly have lived as long as I have if I hadn't known that!

We were also introduced to Murray Code, where we had to read a five-hole tape, the holes punched across it, each letter being represented by a different set of holes. Figures were conveyed after a punched line that was the equivalent of a figure shift. It was a modification of Émile Baudot's 5-bit code, invented in 1870, which also became the basis of the International Telegraph Alphabet No.1.

Murray, bless his little cotton socks, had improved and modified it in 1901 into the version we were presented with.

That took a bit or learning, but all of us mastered it in time for the finals.

Another thing we had to learn was the Phonetic Alphabet – the British one, used before and throughout the war, and, I think, so much superior to the American one which superseded it. The words were pithy and easy to recognise, even through tremendous static: ABLE BAKER CHARLIE DOG EASY FOX GEORGE HOW

ITEM JIG KING LOVE MIKE NAN OBOE PETER ROGER QUEENIE SUGAR TARE UNCLE VICTOR WILLIAM X-RAY ZEBRA. I could never see the sense in changing that to another which replaced JIG with the awkward JULIETTE, UNCLE with UNIFORM, QUEENIE with QUEBEC, and particularly FOX with FOXTROT. Progress? Not in my book!

As far as the most important bit of the course was concerned, the Morse, about half the class reached 25wpm by the end of the final week.

Shortly before that time I was sent by the instructor one morning to see a civilian in a little room at Station Headquarters. His whole manner made me think of cloaks and daggers, and his name, or at least the name he gave me, backed up that impression: Brown. I suppose it was marginally more inventive than Smith or Jones.

He asked me a lot of questions about my family and my life and education up to that time, plus some others that made little sense to me, but which I later realised were relevant to the positive vetting process.

Then he told me that I had been selected for potential extra training, leading to a special job, but first I had to go to RAF Cheadle for an interview with a Wing Commander W.G. Swannborough, whom I later found out was Winco Retd.

We were given ten days' leave at the end of the course, and most of the lads and lasses were given postings. Mine would depend on the result of the interview.

I had saved a bit of cash at Compton and after two days at home bought myself a second-hand BSA 350cc motorcycle, my third such vehicle, the first having been a 125cc Francis Barnett that would just about reach 40mph on a good day, going downhill with a following strong wind, and the second a Triumph 250, which I had sold before going overseas.

The BSA would certainly not be my last bike, in a love affair with that mode of transport which lasted for forty years and included such iconic models as the Ariel Foursquare, the Norton International, the water-cooled Fox and the single cylinder, twin-port, Rudge Sports Special, with several Triumphs and different size Beesas thrown in for good measure, despite having as my main conveyance a motor car. When I see what some of those bikes are worth now it makes me wish I'd had a crystal ball that had told me to keep them.

Coming into possession of a Japanese model four years ago and still having my licence to ride one, I rode it into Norwich and back, deciding long before arriving home from the ten-mile ride that I would never ever do it again. The near misses from drivers who seemed oblivious to my presence on the road taught me quickly how bloody dangerous motorcycling is nowadays. I'll get in and close the door, thank you.

It was so different in those days, with so little traffic on the roads, and I'd decided to ride to Cheadle, to avoid the dreadful walk across town from Peterborough East, the end of the line for the East Anglian train, to Peterborough North, where the connection to the Midlands came in; at the time the only way to get across country by rail from the wilds of Norfolk.

Motor-cycling clothing was then not anything like as efficient as it is nowadays, and my suit was of the thick, wax-impregnated, cloth type. The leather helmet and the goggles were ex-aircrew; not exactly the ideal things for the job. Nicely collectable now though.

One such helmet came into my possession from a house clearance about five years ago and I advertised it on eBay. It sold for £55. There were so many around in 1952 that they were merely thrown away.

On the day of the interview I set off at five am in a fairly heavy drizzle. I had on my uniform, and for extra warmth had wrapped my RAF three-coloured silk scarf around my neck, unaware that it was not colour fast.

By the time I reached Peterborough the waxed suit was soaked through, and I could feel that I was sitting in a pool of water. My goggles kept steaming up, and for much of the time I pushed them up onto my forehead and had to keep blinking as the raindrops got heavier and heavier.

About forty miles after Peterborough, with the rain now slashing down, I leant the bike over into a sharp bend and blinked as I came out of it.

The next thing I knew, I was on my side about thirty feet into a deeply ploughed field, with the bike between my legs and the engine still running, the back tyre throwing gouts of muddy soil into the air.

There had been a second sharp bend following the first, and luckily for me there had been an open gateway that I had sailed through.

I heard a hooter and looked towards the gateway as I slapped the bike out of gear.

A lorry was stopped there with an open-mouthed driver staring at me. I realised I had just missed colliding with him too.

He recovered his composure and shouted, 'Are you all right, mate?'

I shouted 'Yes', and he drove off, shaking his head.

Now I was not only just soaked through, but covered in mud too. Just perfect for an interview with a senior officer.

The rest of the journey was miserable, and my eyes stung, since the goggles were useless, but at least the heavy rain washed off the mud.

I booked in at RAF Cheadle, and a sympathetic corporal found me some dry civilian trousers and a jacket at least one size too small and took my wet uniform to dry before a fire. Looking in the mirror I found one thing I could not disguise: my neck, and the collar and top of my RAF shirt, which were now red, white and blue. The colours remained in my skin for almost a week, despite rigorous scrubbing. Those colours had run fast enough from the scarf, but they had decided that their new home would be more permanent.

I must have looked a damned strange sight when I presented myself for interview that afternoon at what the locals called The Big House – Woodhead Hall, in the hamlet of Hammersley Hayes, but not a thing was said about it, and my interviewer appeared not to notice. I thought at the time that he must have been tipped off.

Wing Commander Swannborough was, basically, the senior recruiting officer for all RAF 'Y' staff, a highly intelligent and interesting man who, it was rumoured, had so much power that he had once had a troopship returned to port to take a man off. Known affectionately as 'Swanney', he was fanatically proud of 'his' service.

He informed me that I was suitable for the 'Y' service and that I must never, for the entire course of my life, ever divulge that fact, nor mention the sacred letter, on pain of death or worse. How times have changed!

My orders were to return to Cheadle at the end of my leave and begin work in the 'hut on the hill', a wooden construction with a set room big enough for around twenty operators, which had a civilian supervisor and another civilian, Don, in charge. He had a tiny office at the other end of the hut from the set room. Above the hut an HF aerial serving all the sets was strung between two tall pylons, each guyed with three hawsers leading down to massive eyed bolts in three foot cubes of concrete, weighing around two tons. On the other side of each concrete block, a shorter hawser led from another eyed bolt down to the anchorages – concrete pads in the ground.

RAF Cheadle was one of the smallest RAF stations in existence – just half a dozen huts on each side of a slope, a small NAAFI, an even smaller mess, and a guardroom. The CO was Flight Lieutenant MacWhirter, a really good officer, who was kind of a father figure to his subordinates, most of them anyway, but more of that shortly.

'The Potteries', as the area is locally known, came as something of an environmental shock. For a start, the accent and local word usage was most strange, and it took a couple of weeks before it was relatively easy to understand what was being said to one, and the area seemed drab to me, with the rows and rows of similar, sad-looking houses, but the lasses were flirtatious, and that gave me and the other newcomers encouragement.

I and a couple of mates visited Stoke-on-Trent and some of the other towns and villages around Cheadle, looking for talent and entertainment.

In the hut on the hill I was introduced for the first time to the HRO radio receiver, a superheterodyne (there's that word again) set that covered a bandwidth of 1.7 Megaherz to 30 Megaherz, by using four plug-in coils, which had graphs that could be correlated to the micrometer readout to find the tuned frequency. The boffins had found that using coils gave greater sensitivity, lower noise and less signal loss than receivers using band-switching circuits. The story goes that it was originally going to be called the HOR, with the obvious unfortunate connotations, since some senior wag at the factory reckoned it was a 'Hell of a rush' to get the thing out on the market, but good sense prevailed, and it was modified to a 'Helluva rush order', and hence the HRO was born.

Later in life, the Russians, no doubt tipped off to our use of that receiver by people like the spy, Dougie Britten, often changed frequency from one band to another, and I could imagine some little Soviet operator grinning diabolically as he thought about his British counterparts frantically changing coils because of his actions. After a minute or so he would often change back, or to a different frequency on the original coil. Great sport, and done away with ten years or so later, when all RAF 'Y' service receivers were changed to the newer Racal RA17.

Using the HRO I was given the task of intercepting a part of the Polish Air Force.

The 'skeds' – the schedule of working that was expected – was printed on a board beside the receiver, and each day at set times the control station would come on the air for a few minutes and send five-figure encoded groups, which probably contained such earth-shattering information as the current stores holding of 'caps, large-peaked, Polish officers for the use of' or the set cookhouse menus for that day at all their airfields.

The ways in which the operators handled their Morse keys – referred to in the trade as their 'fists', were quite identifiable, with no two operators sending in the same way, like fingerprints in the ether, and those of the three control station operators were excellent, but on the rare occasions that I heard an outstation reply the operator was badly trained, with slow speed and frequent errors.

For a couple of months it seemed that the Polish Air Force was doing no flying; it was so quiet, and then, for a week, every one of their nets was working flat out as they carried out an extended exercise.

After that it was back to the boredom.

Boredom which one day went out of the window with a bang!

It was a sticky hot summer day, with a wall-to-wall blue sky, and nothing much was doing on the air.

There were nineteen of us working the sets.

Suddenly, the supervisor poked his head round the door and warned, 'Thunderstorm coming, boys. Switch off.'

Thunderstorm? He must be joking, I thought, but orders is orders, so, like all the others, I turned off the receiver at the mains and pulled the earphones down until they were round my neck, as you do.

Half an hour or so went by, which we spent chatting about this and that, with not the slightest sign of a cloud or the sound of thunder.

The next thing I knew I was coming round, lying on the floor. I opened my eyes to see every other operator either lying dormant or beginning to move.

Pulling myself up to my feet seemed to take forever, and my co-ordination was all to pot.

My head felt as if it had been hit with baseball bat.

The other lads were in a similar state, and it took a while before we were anything like fully compos mentis again.

The air was full of smoke, rising from every piece of wiring in the room.

I realised then what had happened – a bolt of lightning out of that clear blue sky had hit the aerial above us.

Had we left our earphones over our ears we would have been deaf for life, and we were bloody lucky to be alive.

I don't know which of us began it, but someone started laughing, and it was infectious. Suddenly, all of us were falling about, looking at each other and laughing hysterically because we were still alive. At least, if we were not, the smoking set room did not look like anyone's idea of Heaven, or Hell, if it came to that.

As the laughter lessened, I suddenly thought of Don, alone in his little office along the corridor, and moved towards the door, followed by a couple of the others.

The corridor was also full of smoke, making us cough, and the telephone and other wires that had been fed along the tops of the walls had melted and were all smoking.

We reached Don's office and saw him sitting there, staring directly ahead of him into space, totally unaware that we were standing in his doorway.

In front of him, on his desk, his old GPO telephone was a misshapen mass of black plastic, from which a thin column of smoke was rising.

I went around his desk and shook his shoulder.

He turned his head slowly and peered short-sightedly at me.

'Whaaa…?'

I shook his shoulder harder, 'Don, are you all right?'

He seemed to come to and asked, 'What happened?'

I told him we'd been struck by lightning, and he tried to get up, but sat back down again.

Gradually, we came back to some form of normality and tried to take stock.

The innards of every set in the place had been destroyed, and not one wire in the building remained intact.

We went outside.

The two pylons still stood, but the antenna wires that had been strung between them were missing entirely, and the guy hawsers hung loose.

What astonished us most was that there was not a sign of those huge concrete blocks.

The largest piece of concrete we could find was less than two inches in diameter.

The bolt of lightning had run down the hawsers into the eye-bolts and had jumped across from one to the other, blowing those blocks of concrete asunder as if they had been hit by a tactical atomic weapon. The electrical charge, travelling down the hawsers as the lines of least resistance, had probably saved our lives, by taking most of the power out of it.

It seemed that the Cheadle intercept station would be out of action for some considerable time, but amazingly, with the help of a small army of experts, it was up and running again five days later.

I wondered if the Polish Air Force, no doubt informed of the problem, would have carried out a massive exercise while we erks were unable to intercept them.

We enjoyed some unexpected free time, which we used to our advantage.

Returning one evening from the village, I was passing the guardroom, singing quietly and tunelessly one of the songs from the current hit parade, when a voice from inside shouted, 'Hey, you! Come 'ere!'

One of the acting-unpaid-uneducated-unwanted corporal 'snowdrops' – a Service Policeman - came out, looking angry and full of importance.

He made me come to attention and then astonished me by putting me on a charge: "Conduct prejudicial to good order and discipline in the Royal Air Force.'

I tried to ask what I had done wrong, but he told me to shut up and ordered me to report the next morning for the hearing and disappeared back inside the little guardroom.

I was stunned to say the least. All I'd been doing was singing; something I've done all my life and still do, to the annoyance of anyone who is near me, since the same song tends to go on all day, and my wife does occasionally say, 'Change the record, darling', but I've always been a happy soul, and that's the way I express my happiness.

The next morning, with boots, badges and buttons shined, I turned up for the charge to be heard and was marched in, coming to a smart attention in front of Flight Lieutenant MacWhirter.

The corporal SP read out the charge, and MacWhirter looked at me questioningly.

'This is a very serious charge.' He said, 'What have you got to say for yourself?'

I shrugged, 'I was only singing, sir.'

He looked puzzled, 'Singing? At the top of your voice?'

'No, sir, just to myself.'

'Oh, I see. You were singing a dirty rugby song then?'

'No, sir. I think it was Nat King Cole's *"Too Young"*.

There was a long, pregnant pause before MacWhirter turned to the SP, his eyebrows raised and his voice soft and smooth as molasses, 'Is that correct, Corporal Glastonbury?'

'Yes, *sir*!' Glastonbury belted out the reply.

He'd been watching too many films featuring American marines.

I watched MacWhirter's face turn mottled with anger. He breathed heavily a couple of times and then gritted out, 'Corporal Glastonbury, when my men are singing, they are happy. When my men are happy, I am happy. But at this moment I am very unhappy – with you! You have wasted all our time here this morning with this ridiculously frivolous charge, and if you ever bring such a charge in front of me again, I shall ensure that you spend the rest of your service painting the stones outside a guardroom in Outer Mongolia! Charge dismissed!'

To me he said, 'I can only offer my apologies for the behaviour of one of my NCOs. This charge will not go on your record. Please do carry on singing.'

I made a point of singing every time I went past the guardroom after that, looking into the window and grinning, but I was careful not to contravene any of the King's Regulations. I knew Glastonbury would delight in charging me with something that would stick.

It came as no surprise when only a couple of weeks later my favourite snowdrop was suddenly posted.

One of the Naafi girls was off sick, and the manager employed a local girl to take her place for a week. She was an attractive blonde, only five feet three, with curly hair and lots of freckles.

We hit it off immediately, and I asked her out.

She agreed, and after work the next day I met her and asked what she would like to do.

It was November, and a bit cold. We both wore overcoats.

There was little to do in town, so we decided to go for a walk up the dark hill behind the town, both aware of our intentions. Every few yards we stopped and snogged, becoming worked up, and tried to consummate our short relationship against a fence; an undertaking that just didn't work because of the difference in our heights and our relative incompetence. The ground was soaking wet after several days of heavy rain.

We moved on, hoping against hope to find somewhere conducive to our requirements, and walking along the darkened roadway stumbled over something that almost made us fall.

I smoked in those days and struck a match, which went out almost immediately, but gave us a glimpse of a body, lying on the road.

I bent low and struck several more, each of which went out quickly, but it was obvious that whoever lay there was dead, and that there was blood all over the face. The hairs on the back of my neck were standing out straight. My first dead body, and it was dark and scary. The girl was clinging tightly to my arm, even more scared than I was.

Imagine how we felt. What to do?

There were two houses fifty yards or so further up the road, only one of them with a light showing.

We ran up and I pounded on the door.

No one came.

I pounded some more and we heard movement inside.

The door opened a fraction, and we saw a man even shorter than my companion, with one of the ugliest faces I'd ever seen. In the heightened state we were in he looked like an angry Troll.

'What do you want?' He growled.

I explained about the body and he tried to shut the door.

I put my foot in it and asked, 'Have you got a torch we can borrow?'

He swore, but turned around and felt inside the pocket of a coat hanging in the hall.

'Bring it straight back.'

'Have you got a phone, to call the police?'

'No.'

The door stayed open and he watched us as we retraced our steps to where the body lay.

The batteries in the torch were almost flat, but by its weak light we looked at the body.

It was a very lifelike male mannequin, dressed in a suit, complete with a shirt and tie, and someone had painted 'blood' all over the face with red paint.

That was when I remembered that Guy Fawkes Day was only a couple of days away.

Someone had a bizarre sense of humour.

Though the road was used very little, the first driver coming across the body would have had hysterics similar to the ones we had enjoyed.

I picked up the mannequin and threw it into the hedge.

We returned the torch, which was grabbed by a hand before the door slammed. The guy had not even asked about our find, which made me wonder if he was behind the 'joke'.

The shock gradually wore off, and we went back to 'trying' – half a dozen times, in fact, on the way back to camp, in different locations, without success.

Becoming desperate, with booking-in time fast approaching, in a narrow alley behind some houses not far from the guardroom, I did a Sir Walter Raleigh with my greatcoat, placing the inside on the wet ground, not realising that the path was mainly brick-dust. When I left the RAF twenty years later that brick dust could still be seen, despite the garment having been dry-cleaned numerous times. Ah, memories!

Satisfied at last, we parted just before the gate.

On my return to the billet, I was hardly through the door when I was grabbed, badly roughed up and interrogated by my then best friend, an older man, who had left one of the other Services to join the RAF. Up to that moment he had been all sweetness and light and a great pal.

I refused to give any information, but he obviously knew from the state of my greatcoat what had happened.

I had something of an epiphany the next day, learning with a severe jolt something important about human relationships and trust.

It was the first time someone I had classed as a good friend would betray me, but it would not be the last by any means.

He grabbed the girl's arm as she passed us in the Naafi the next day and suggested in a loud voice in front of a couple of dozen other lads that instead of wasting her charms – and he didn't mince words - on a callow youth like me, she should give them to a mature man instead. Tears leapt into her eyes as she pulled herself away, watched by all the others in the room. I could have killed him. If you are still alive and reading this at the age of ninety-two, you old bastard, just be aware that I have never forgiven you for the totally unnecessary embarrassment you caused that charming young girl.

Naturally, she assumed that I had been bragging about our encounter and would not even look at me from then on.

Her week at the Naafi was up a couple of days later, and I never saw her again.

I have fond memories of her to this day, and would have dearly liked to apologise to her.

I expected to spend quite a while at Cheadle, but shortly after that incident I was told that I was being sent back to Compton Bassett for re-training to become a Telegraphist IIA, learning the skill of typing.

Compton was just as dreary as before, but I felt like an old hand, and used one of the tricks I had used the last time to avoid the weekly parades:

volunteering to clear the waste paper baskets in the classrooms before the day's lessons began. Pay parades, of course, I always attended. A thing of the distant past now, they were often the highlight of the week, though long-winded. Even if your name began with an 'A' you had to fall back into line and wait the process through to the end. On some stations, you were allowed to fall out after being paid, but not at Compton at that time.

The 3-card brag schools were always in session on pay nights, and the NAAFI's sales of beer hit their weekly high.

Typing, I found, was not as easy as learning to send and receive Morse.

We were taught on the old sit-up-and-beg L.C.Smith typewriter, always called an Elsie Smith, of course, and the keyboard was covered up by a metal sheet, under which one's hands were inserted.

We began with the QWERTY set and progressed very gradually until we were typing with the full keyboard.

As with Morse, you reached a stage where any increase in speed seemed to be impossible, and I used the same trick as I had with Morse, typing nothing but mixed letter and figure groups instead of plain language.

Something important happened shortly after beginning the course: I fell in love for the first time in my life.

Eileen was delightful. She was blonde, five feet eight and slimly built, with a lovely disposition, and she fell for me as I did for her. She was a virgin, but not a blushing violet, having been brought up in one of the less salubrious parts of Hull, and we discussed openly the sex thing. It was something she was saving for marriage, she said, and I respected her for that.

We were inseparable, and it made the time go quickly and pleasantly. Like me, she loved dancing.

She was also doing the typing course, but was not in the 'Y' Service.

Towards the end of the course I took her home for a long weekend, to meet my family. I was that serious about her, and we had been talking marriage.

My mother thought Eileen was a great girl, very down to earth and ready to pitch in with any work. I said I wanted to marry her, and received instant approval. In her turn Eileen thought mother was one of the nicest women she had ever met, and wished she had a family like mine. She was right about my mother, who was a quite wonderful woman in many ways.

We spent a pleasant day on the Saturday, dancing in the evening at the Samson and Hercules ballroom in Norwich.

Sunday was just as its name suggests, a grand day with full sunshine, and I took Eileen out onto the wild area behind our bungalow to the lakes, as we called them – gravel pits which had been excavated and then abandoned. I had always used them as my own private fishery and was disgusted some years later when I visited to fish there and found that they had been sold en bloc to a London fishing club and were all fenced off, with 'Strictly Private' notices all over the place.

We'd taken a blanket with us and found a lovely spot in the sun.

A lot of kissing went on, and then intimate fondling, both of us ready to throw caution to the wind.

Despite good intentions, it was obvious what was imminently about to happen, but suddenly my eye caught a movement behind a grassy bank, and when I turned to look I saw a small grubby face peering over it.

I shouted, 'Go away!', but in seconds we were surrounded by six of the urchin offspring of a local didicoy family, the eldest no more than ten, chanting absolutely filthy remarks and demanding to be allowed to watch. That family was infamous in the area, the unmarried mother regularly producing a child every nine or ten months, in a fashion one of my German maids later described as 'Wie Schüsse aus einem Revolver."

The moment ruined, we headed home after some swearing on my part at the still chanting kids, unsure if we were pleased or not that we had not been able to succumb to temptation.

I think it was disappointment on my part that caused my flare up.

It was something small and insignificant that was said, but my mother had always been able to wind me up, and she did so that day.

I flew off the handle, shouting at her as I stormed out of the house, knowing that I was totally at fault and was showing my very worst side to Eileen.

When I returned two hours later there was nothing said, but my sweetheart ignored me.

We left to catch the train in mid-afternoon, and we had hardly exchanged a word.

Back at Compton, as I tried to kiss her by the WAAF lines, Eileen turned her head to one side and told me matter-of-factly, 'I won't see you any more, Tony. It's over. Your mother is a wonderful lady, and the way you shouted at her was dreadful. I could not possibly marry you.'

She turned and walked out of my life. She was such a wonderful girl that I feel we might have married and still be together now if I had not been so much of a jerk.

I did not enjoy the last couple of weeks at Compton, and just lost myself in the work.

Typing nothing but letter and figure groups was dreadfully boring, but I stuck at it before going back to what the others had been doing all along, and found that although I had only improved by six or seven wpm with the groups I had jumped almost twenty words a minute with plain language, in a similar manner to that in which I had improved my Morse speed. I went back to the hard stuff for another increase, and easily reached the required speed for pass-out, after a very bumpy start. That type of practice, though I didn't know it at the time, would be a good grounding for a job I would be employed on for almost a year at another RAF station a while later.

CHAPTER THREE

My posting came through to 755 Signals Unit, RAF Uetersen, near Hamburg, part of what we liked to call Second TAF – Second Tactical Air Force, though the title had been changed to British Air Force of Occupation.

First of all, a week's embarkation leave, during which I met and dated a couple of times the girl who would become my first wife, but at the time it was merely a visit to the cinema, thank God not showing '*Hellzapoppin'*, and an evening's dancing. It was not serious enough that we were going to write to one another, and I also dated two of her mates during that week, favouring one called Patty, who was a game girl and made the end of that holiday very memorable. I am smiling now as I remember it!

It was quite an experience, catching the boat train at Harwich for the voyage to the Hook of Holland. Army officialdom made everything more difficult than it needed to be, but eventually everyone was on board and 'accounted for'.

It was a rough crossing, with spew flying everywhere, and I went up on deck and stayed forrard, where the air was clean and very bracing, but I preferred to shiver.

Later, when all the sickies had gone to lie down, I went to the canteen and had a satisfying meal of liver and bacon. There was plenty for seconds and I indulged.

Everywhere smelt bad, but it didn't put me off. My early years spent bobbing about in boats had paid off.

Holland was just as I expected it to be, much like parts of my home county of Norfolk, but with more windmills, and northern Germany was not much different.

Eventually, after changing trains three times, I arrived late in the evening at Uetersen, a camp which seemed at first sight to have nothing to recommend it.

I couldn't have been more wrong.

It had begun as a glider airfield for sports enthusiasts in 1933 and was taken over by an expanding Luftwaffe and built out in 1936 to house various units of the German Air Force during the Second World War, and their personnel had it good.

What astonished me immediately was being housed in a well built brick barracks with, unbelievably, double glazing and central heating – both virtually unheard of in England at that time.

After Compton Bassett it was like the Lord Mayor's Show after the honey cart.

The closeness of Hamburg was a big bonus. The variety and availability of attractions made the city a Mecca for the troops, but the first visit was an eye-opener.

Four square miles of the city was flat, with not one brick standing on another – a sight that left me breathless with the enormity of the result from *Operation Gomorrah,* conducted by the RAF and the USAF, which had created a firestorm that killed and wounded 80,000 of the citizens of the city, and caused a million to flee.

Nevertheless, during the years following the war, the rest of the city had been more or less re-built, and there were enough bars and nightspots to keep any airman happy. Especial care had been taken to re-create the Reeperbahn, the mile-long

Hamburg red light district, where any taste could be catered for.

Though I had come across prostitutes in many different parts of the world I had never been tempted to use one. Not for fear of disease, though that is always a factor a man should consider, but because of a rule I had made inflexible regarding my sex life: my partner's needs would always be more important than mine.

In my late teens, I had read the translation of a very ancient Chinese book on lovemaking, in one part of which the advice was given: *"No matter what the circumstances, when you are coupling with a woman, it is imperative that you ensure that she is completely satisfied, either at the same time as or before you, and, if necessary, even to the detriment of your own pleasure. Her satisfaction should be your guiding star and will give you the greatest delight. For her part, she will believe you unique and will love you forever"*.

The last sentence is somewhat hyperbolic, but nevertheless, there is truth in it.

It made a great deal of sense to me, and I have always followed that advice and can state with absolute conviction that it was the best I have ever received.

In fact, on three occasions it worked too well, and I had great difficulty extracting myself from the relationships.

Those old Chinese guys knew a thing or two!

Quite apart from that, cold, clinical sex with someone for whom I felt no affection, and who had none for me, held about as much appeal as jumping into a bath full of needle sharp ice cubes.

I had never before seen women selling themselves from what could only be described as 'shop windows'. And some of those women were by any manner of judging beauties. Coffee being something the Germans just could not get hold of at that time, a jar of Nescafe – black market price 40 marks - would have bought you any one of them. Though it made me sad, wondering how many of them had been unwillingly forced into that life, seeing them like that was an experience I would not have wanted to miss. Nowadays, of course, the Reeperbahn is a heavily hyped, glittering place, which is on every visiting tourist's 'must see' list.

After that first visit I gave it a miss and frequented the bars down by the river, where the beer was cheaper.

I don't know how others have found their first experience of Germany, but mine was the distinctive, different smell – a smell of strange tobacco, from the short, stubby cigars that everyone seemed to smoke. Another thing I noticed that one did not see in the UK was the use of red and black chevron signs at the sides of the road to indicate where vehicles should drive when entering closed off areas, like barracks or hospitals.

I'd expected to have difficulty with the language, but found that if I spoke Norfolk dialect they could understand me perfectly well, and I could understand them. I had many long discussions with other drinkers in the bars I frequented, about all sorts of things. I was enjoying myself.

It made me want to learn the language properly, and I began to make a real effort to do so.

What I did not realise was that the language I was learning was not the language of the average German, but Plattdeutsch or Niederdeutsch – Low German, only spoken in that area; a mixture of

German and Dutch, influenced heavily by the trade with Eastern England over hundreds of years.

I hardly had time to get to know the place too well, because after just three months of working in a centrally heated, double glazed set-room I was sent for and asked if I would like to be employed on Codes and Cyphers.

Would I? Imagining that it would be all cloak and dagger stuff I volunteered straight away and found myself sent on a one-week course to Bletchley Park, where I first of all learnt to use a Typex machine, of the type I would be using when I went back to Germany. I did also learn a whole lot about codes and ciphers, including their interesting history and early versions, most of the information totally unnecessary for the job I was about to do, but I was introduced to something that I would use a great deal on a later posting: the 'Double-Shuffle Board' – an intriguing way of double-enciphering a message using, for example, in the first instance, a one-time pad, and then re-enciphering it. The result was totally secure, unless the code-cracker knew the settings. There were two plastic boards, the rear one sliding, giving an entirely different set of figures to those from the original encryption.

One other thing occurred: I was made to sign another document regarding the Secrets Acts, and was elevated from '*Secret Codeword*' to '*Top Secret Codeword*' clearance. In my new job I would be handling end-product.

Whereas the Air Force generally used merely the classification of a document, the 'Y' service always employed a codeword, which followed the grading, and was generally a word from a series – the names of gemstones or musical instruments, for example, like '*Secret Sapphire*' or '*Top Secret Flute*'.

I was to see many changes of codeword during my twenty years 'in the game'.

When I returned to Uetersen I found I had been posted to RAF Hambühren and, wonder of wonder, given my substantive corporal's tapes.

A couple of years after that, in July 1955, the entire unit from Uetersen moved to Hambühren. It had been felt that its location, so close to the border with East Germany, made it vulnerable if Warsaw Pact Forces invaded. Hambühren, in its turn, would eventually be left by the RAF and handed over to the West German Feldmelderregiment 71, one of their three ELINT intercept stations – their *Funkmessbeobachtungsstellen.*

I was met at the railway station in Celle, the large town close to my new unit, and driving out there had a chance to look at the countryside.

It was absolutely flat, with hardly a dwelling along the five-mile route. The soil was acidic and low in nutrients, and the fir trees growing as far as the eye could see were poor, spindly specimens.

As at Uetersen, the accommodation at Hambühren was double-glazed and centrally heated.

The cipher section was next to one of the set rooms, but could not be accessed except by the personnel working there, a couple of technicians who were Top Secret Codeword cleared and three of the officers.

There were no windows to give daylight, and only an extractor fan in the outer wall to do something – but not much – to change the air.

The improved Typex enciphering machines we used – the improved Mark 22, introduced in

1950, also gave off heat, being powered by electricity, and we often worked in vests and underpants and still sweated.

The Typex, or Type X, was originally a version of the German commercial Enigma machine, though far superior; so superior, in fact, that the Germans, after they had captured a couple of Typex and investigated them, decided that the output was 'unbreakable', and gave up their efforts.

Our machine was also superior in other ways: it needed only one operator, whereas the Enigma needed two, and each message had to be hand-written, enciphered, and transmitted by Morse Code.

When it was received it had to be deciphered and written out again.

The Typex automatically enciphered and transmitted the message.

The first production models of the Typex were produced in 1937. Like the Enigma, it was a rotor machine, but had five rotors, compared to the three or four in the Enigma. The mechanics who serviced them were hard pressed to keep them spotlessly clean and efficiently working. One thing that was necessary was for the rotor contacts to be lubricated only with Vaseline, since using oil might cause arcing, though oil was used for other parts of the apparatus.

The machines we were using, geared to around 50 words per minute, were much improved on the early models, on which only 20wpm was possible, and all of us could send for eight hours at a time, using perfect rhythm, at that higher speed.

The perfect rhythm was necessary, since the key, at the end of every tap, was locked electronically for several thousandths of a second before another key could be pressed, and we had it off to a 'T'.

One day, when I'd been working there for about six months, a team of American operators visited from Bad Aibling. After they had entered the door they stood open-mouthed, watching us work. All their messages were typed up on Creed tape-producing machines, where any mistake could be erased by typing in Xs. We often saw large lengths of incoming tape with foot-long lengths of five holes across them.

The Americans could just not believe that we typed the five-figure groups online.

The shifts worked were 'two-on, two-off' – morning and evening shift on one day, and afternoon and night shift the next, followed by a sleeping day and a free day. The body never had a chance to get used to any one of them, and all of us would have preferred to be on just one shift, even if it was permanent nights. We did suggest it, but it was turned down.

We were all heavy drinkers, and swallowed a lot of spirits every evening when we were not on duty, but one lad was a real piss-artist and he drank only rum and coke.

Imagine to yourself walking into an almost sealed room at five to eight in the morning to relieve someone who has been sweating and farting stale rum all night, with no chance to open a window or leave a door open! The stink almost knocked one over.

We tried to get him to change tipple on the evenings before he went on duty at midnight, but to no avail. Rum was his poison of choice, and he intended sticking with it.

The code and cipher room was officially staffed with thirteen men, but when I arrived there were only ten, including me, and near the time when I left there were just six of us.

We sent on average two million code groups a month by hand, not by tape, and our average mistake rate was three mistakes per month. Though it sounds incredible, it is perfectly true.

Now and again I had the necessity to encode a particular type of message using the Double Shuffle Board, giving me the chance to use the skill acquired at Bletchley Park. I became a dab hand at it.

We frequently had lectures about security, and the fact that the Russians were not that far away was regularly impressed upon us. The powers that be must have taken it seriously, because we had four sledge hammers on the inventory of our little section, to smash up the machines in case of invasion!

It was in the standing orders on the back of our door.

I had some annual leave to come, and with two friends took advantage of the wonderful facilities offered at the Forces' Leave Centre in the town of Bad Harzburg, situated at the northern foot of the Harz mountains, on the edge of the Harz National Park, through which the River Radau flows, a minor tributary of the River Oker. East of it is the boundary between the states of Lower Saxony and Saxony-Anhalt, which had at one time been the Inner German Border.

Bad Harzburg Leave Centre closed three years later, but during the years that it operated, thousands of servicemen stationed in Germany enjoyed wonderful sporting leaves there, where, for the princely sum of nine old pence a day – less than five pence in modern coinage - one had bed and full board – the meals huge and of excellent quality - and the use of appropriate clothing, skis and skiing equipment, a variety of sledges and ice skates, and the free use of the ski-lift and ice rink. We were even given rail warrants to get there and back.

It was like a different world; snow four feet deep, the town looking like a Christmas card scene as we approached.

We took full advantage, learning the skill of skiing from a grizzled, veteran instructor, one of several employed by the Leave Centre, and practiced that art every day we were there except one, when we spent almost four hours in the morning dragging a huge sled to the top of the nearby mountain and three of the most exhilarating and dangerous minutes of our lives hurtling headlong and virtually out of control back downhill at a speed that must have been near terminal velocity, missing so many huge fir trees by mere inches that it seemed impossible we could reach the bottom alive – a stupidity never to be repeated!

We did it again in the afternoon.

It was, without doubt, one of the most memorable leaves of my service, and I would have loved to repeat it, but demand was so great that only one visit per person was allowed.

My brother, two and a half years younger than I, had joined the RAF on a three-year contract, gone to Compton and followed my footsteps into the 'Y' Service.

One could, in those days, claim a close relative to serve on the same station, and I did that very thing.

Patrick arrived a couple of months later and went to work in the set room, but he confided that he did not want to sign on in the RAF and fancied becoming a copper in Civvy Street.

Every man to his own particular brand of poison, I thought, and agreed that if that is what he wanted to do, then he should do it.

He was only on the unit for five months before going home for demob.

Had he stayed in the RAF, he might, with luck, have reached the dizzy heights of Flight Sergeant or even Warrant Officer, but during his service in the police he spent a year each at the Police College at Bramshill and the internationally acclaimed German Police Academy, attended London University and achieved a law degree, reached the rank of Superintendent, retired after serving 38 years on half pay, cost-of-living coupled, and with a huge lump sum, and immediately landed a job with the Forces Legal Department, having entered the Civil Service with the rank of Higher Executive Officer. He then returned to Germany, where his pay and overseas living allowances were astronomical. He was also entitled to the cheap petrol and other perks given to Forces personnel, of course. He carried on with that until he was forced to finally retire at the age of 72 with an even greater pension, and then began teaching German businessmen English, at a phenomenal amount of Deutschmarks per hour. He is doing that still.

I often wonder if he made the right decision. They did, after all, offer him his corporal's tapes if he would sign on!

My German was coming on apace, and I seized every opportunity to speak to native speakers, particularly those who spoke English and could explain things about the language.

One of those native speakers was Gertie, one of the four German NAAFI girls.

Being very kind I will say that she was not a beauty. About eight years older than I was, she had straggly blonde hair that no matter what she did never looked cared for, although she was a meticulously clean person. She had been injured by an icicle which fell from a roof when she was young and the scar that ran down her forehead from the hairline had distorted the area around one eye, making it appear that the eye was out of alignment.

I was not in the least put off by her appearance, and we spent many hours when she was not busy speaking German.

One day, she asked if I could get into the NAAFI compound, which was strictly out of bounds to us, one evening.

With only German language learning in mind (honestly!), I said I could, although it meant climbing over a ten-foot high steel gate.

We arranged a time just after dark and I did as she suggested.

We sat down at the dining table, where the other three girls were finishing their meal. One was Freda, the girl who always stayed in the kitchen and never came to the counter or spoke to any of the airmen; in fact hardly spoke at all; a younger girl than the others, much overweight, with a fat face and a permanent grimace.

When she had left with the others to go to their rooms, Gertie told me that Freda had been raped by over twenty Russian soldiers when she was twelve, and it had left her permanently affected mentally.

The girls had been sharing a bottle of wine, and we finished that off. Gertie then produced another one and that soon followed the first.

I seem to remember that at least two more were emptied over the next couple of hours, Gertie becoming more beautiful with each glassful, and then I found myself in bed with her.

It was after two when I crawled under the fence at the place we had made for the use of all of us when we wanted to be out of camp after curfew, and tiptoed up the stairs and into the billet in almost pitch darkness.

I was tiptoeing towards my bed when all the lights were thrown on and I found everyone in the room sitting up in bed, laughing their heads off, throwing pillows and what have you at me and shouting filthy comments. They all knew where I had been.

I was so pissed that I just grinned and went to bed.

The next morning I realised what I had done, but felt only thankful to Gertie, who must have wanted a man very badly.

At morning break, however, it came back to haunt me with a bang.

One of my so-called mates – I'll just call him 'W', stood up on a chair and shouted out as Gertie came out among us to collect empties, 'Cor! How could you screw her, Tony. What an ugly bitch!'

He carried on in the same vein until I knocked him off his chair and would probably have killed him if I had not been restrained by three or four of my other mates.

Poor Gertie did not show herself at the counter for almost a fortnight, and I felt so sorry for her. She did not deserve that treatment.

Getting under the wire to go out after curfew was a general activity, practiced by one and all, and for one very good reason: after the NAAFI closed, we needed yet more booze.

Of course, the fact that one was also flouting Queen's Regulations and holding two fingers up to the 'snowdrops' - a standard sport among servicemen – gave a heady additional sense of adventure.

Someone on a walk one day had come across a kind of rustic pub in the middle of the woods, about half a mile from the camp, called "*Zur Waldhütte*". What it was doing there, since it was not accessible by road and there seemed to be no other habitation within a couple of miles, I could not imagine, but there were always four or five regulars drinking there, so they had to live nearby.

We soon made it our own, and it was full of carousing airmen every night.

The SPs in Celle and on camp knew we were drinking after curfew somewhere and regularly raided the establishments known to them, gnashing their teeth, we heard, because they couldn't find us.

For months we drank in the woods with impunity.

Then, so we were informed by one of our camp SPs, someone had snitched and told them exactly where it was.

More and more of the boys joined in the fun, and there was a large crowd whooping it up happily late one night when suddenly there were shouts and whistles all around the place, as about twenty SPs swooped in.

It was hilarious and would have made a good movie scene.

Bodies were flying about everywhere, diving out of windows, going up the stairs to get out onto the roof, and charging out through the woods.

Two lads were found in the owner's bed, the covers up over their heads.

After they had been dragged out of it the SPs found two more underneath.

I was one of the 'charging into the woods' brigade, and since there were more of us than there were of them, some of us got away.

Out of breath, I stopped behind a tree a few hundred yards away from the pub, thinking that staying immobile was the safest bet, now I'd got beyond the ring of SPs, and then I heard pounding feet as one of the coppers chased another lad.

He caught up with him about twenty feet from where I was hiding, grabbed him and shouted in his ear, 'Right, Sunshine! You're nicked!'

In the thickest Geordie accent I had ever heard, his captive uttered, 'Nix verstehen, mon.' It was priceless.

Needless to say, the *Waldhütte* was regularly patrolled after that, and we had been deprived of our watering hole.

The CO – Squadron Leader W Edwards – must have realised that with the numbers involved any punishment was pointless.

There were so many up on a charge the next morning that the Adjutant, obviously with Edwards' approval, had all the men captured by the SPs paraded in the mess. With scarcely concealed humour, he read them the riot act and gave them a verbal warning.

Only about half a dozen of us had not been caught and had managed to make it back under the fence before the full roll call was made.

Those who had been caught, with the typical sense of the righteous, called us cowards.

I'd become close friends with a fellow corporal who worked alongside me. Ken was six years older than I and had been in a different trade to begin with. He, like many others, had remustered to Teleg II.

He suffered very badly with piles and had to wear sanitary towels all the time.

He told me he had been stationed at RAF Changi, in Singapore, and one day, while crossing the parade ground on the way to the NAAFI, he saw a WAAF officer approaching. He slammed up a smart salute, and at that exact moment his bloody sanitary towel fell out of his shorts.

His description of the WAAF officer's shocked and disbelieving expression had me in fits.

We enjoyed the bars in Celle, but the bus service made it impossible to drink there in the evening, since the last bus left the town just after six.

We needed some form of transport.

Bikes were considered and rejected, but it was not long before the problem was solved.

One of the German labourers I spoke to on most days mentioned that he had a car he wanted to sell. It was a very old one, he said, but I went to look at it.

He was certainly right that it was old. In fact, it had been manufactured in 1934 and was an Opel P4, a sit-up-and-beg, old-fashioned saloon, with maroon paint.

Surprisingly, it started up easily and the engine did not sound too bad.

The labourer wanted it out of his yard, and I purchased it for just one hundred marks.

The brakes were bad, so I bought replacement pads, and Ken and I fitted them.

The problem was that the brakes were then non-existent going forward, but fantastically efficient when reversing. It made us realise that we had fitted them incorrectly, and we disassembled them twice more and refitted them without altering the result. It was a weird puzzle.

I shudder to think about how I drove that vehicle for months, using only the handbrake for stopping. Going down the only hill in the area I had to keep bumping the kerb with the nearside front tyre to aid the handbrake.

How I never hit anything or anybody I just can't imagine. And, of course, I was sometimes better oiled than the car when I was behind that wheel.

Ken and I whooped it up on our time off, finding lots of new places.

Suddenly, however, he began making excuses not to come out with me, and I wondered what I had done. He didn't seem offended, and I could not imagine what had come over him.

Deciding to have it out with him I laid it on the line and asked what was wrong.

Pooh-faced, he admitted he had met a woman and was having an affair with her.

I asked, 'What about your wife?' and he said things had been bad for a year before he'd been posted to Germany, and he'd been considering divorce.

I guess I must have pouted a bit about our lost adventures, and he informed me that Renate had a mate if I was interested – a good looking woman who might be 'available'.

Because my love life had been non-existent since the night with Gertie, I agreed.

We drove into Celle the next evening and met the two women in a bar.

The woman he introduced me to, Gabrielle, was eight years older than I, a good looking blonde with a maternal, though not over-heavy figure, an attractive, roundish face, with generous, laughing lips, and laughter lines around them and her eyes.

She was regarding me with smiling interest, her head slightly to one side.

What she saw must have met with her approval, because she nodded slightly, as if to herself, and took my hand and pressed it in such a way that it felt like a sexual act.

In fact, sex oozed out of her every pore. I was instantly attracted, and the attraction was obviously mutual.

She said, 'If we are going to be friends, I cannot call you something that sounds Italian. Have you a middle name?'

I told her it was Frederick, and she smiled.

'There you are then. Friedrich it will be.'

We drank wine instead of our usual beer, and then Ken said, matter-of-factly, 'We are going back to Renate's place. I'll see you in the morning, Tony.' He grinned, 'Sorry – Friedrich.'

I grinned back and told him okay, I would leave the car outside the pub and meet him there at seven.

Gabrielle and I also left the pub and began walking, but almost immediately she pulled me to her and kissed me as I had never been kissed before, her tongue almost doing a tonsillectomy. It was the sexiest thing I had ever experienced, and it was repeated every few paces.

She lived just a few hundred yards away from the pub, in a flat on the second floor of an old-fashioned block, and by the time we reached the front door of the entrance hall we were both breathing heavily and totally aroused.

She got the front door open and we could wait no more. As we fumbled with each other's clothes she giggled, 'I feel like a schoolgirl on her first date.'

I was astonished, 'Do German schoolgirls do this on their first date?'

'Aaaaahh…that's wonderful…some of them do.'

I could instantly imagine her having done so.

Her kisses almost devoured me and we had steamy sex standing up in the entrance hall. She seemed not to care if one of her neighbours arrived.

We made it up the stairs somehow and reached her bedroom, tearing clothing off each other as we moved across the floor, then fell onto the bed and made love again.

During the night I was woken twice more, and at first light we did it again.

I had fallen heavily in lust.

She told me to stay in bed and went to make coffee. When she carried it in she had with her two younger versions of herself.

Without any embarrassment she said, 'This is Angel; she is twelve, and another Gaby, who's ten. Say hello to Onkel Friedrich.'

Both girls smiled and murmured, 'Guten Morgen, Onkel Friedrich.'

The situation was bizarre in the extreme, and difficult to believe, but I said, 'Guten Morgen' back and returned their smile..

'Off you go and get ready for school.' Gabrielle said, and they trotted off happily.

It was quite incredible: Angel, the older of the two, must have been sexually aware at the age of twelve and known what her mother was doing.

I should have wondered at that moment just how many other Onkels they had greeted in their mother's bed, but other things were occupying my mind at that moment, as Gabrielle threw back the covers and attacked me with her lips, obviously not caring if the girls returned, or knowing that they were too well trained to do so.

It was a madness that would last six months, and a period of my life that I would not have missed for anything in the world.

Gabrielle was a soul-mate. She was a highly educated and intelligent woman, who spoke English better than I did, with an Oxford accent that would have had her accepted in any polite society. She was the PA to a very senior British officer at one of the local Army bases, who allowed her a great deal of leeway in the hours she worked.

She was divorced and told me her husband was always after her, wanting her to come back to him. I could understand why!

With her, my German improved dramatically, and many of the mistakes I had been making were straightened out.

We never made love less than five times a day, and if I wrote here the many ways she knew how to revive my flagging libido and the inventiveness of her lovemaking, these pages would be nothing less than incendiary. She could have written her own definitive version of the Kama Sutra and made Fifty Shades of Grey look merely slightly off-white.

One other thing she did for me was immediately after riding in the Opel for the first time. She was horrified at how I had to use the handbrake to slow down and stop.

She spoke to the old chap who lived below her and introduced him to me.

Otto had worked at the Opel car plant all his life and was now retired.

When I explained the problem he laughed, showing only a dozen teeth when he opened his mouth.

'You've got the springs round the wrong way.' He said.

'But the four springs holding each brake shoe are all the same.' I insisted.

'Not so. I agree, they look the same, but two of them on each brake have got little hooks on one end.'

I was puzzled. He was right. We had noticed them, but had thought that the tiny curls at the ends of the springs were unimportant. They didn't connect with anything, whichever way round they were fitted. Surely that could not cause the problem, could it? Fitted either way round the springs held the brake pads tightly.

He said, 'Come on, let's have a look at them.'

We took the wheels off one by one, jacking each wheel up in turn, and disassembled the brakes.

He nodded to himself when we removed the first brake drum, showed me the tiny difference in the ends of the springs and explained that if they were round the wrong way the brake would not work. He said that because of so many complaints Opel had changed the design of the brakes in 1937.

After he'd helped me change them over I tried braking, and the car stopped on a sixpence. They were just as good when reversing.

I couldn't believe it.

I tried to pay him, but he would not accept anything except a bottle of his favourite tipple, Steinhäger – dreadful rotgut in my opinion.

Gabrielle took me to all sorts of events I would never have dreamed of attending myself, including the ballet, where we sat among many senior officers and their wives.

It was Swan Lake, performed by a British touring company, and included in the cast were three of the top Royal Ballet performers, one of whom was playing Odette. Gabrielle had made several sotto voce comments during the performance, but she had been waiting her time, and when Odette was dying, she exclaimed in a loud, beautifully upper-class voice, 'Oh, I do wish she would get on with it, don't you, *dar*ling?'

The outraged faces that were turned to us had to be seen to be believed.

She was a holy terror in that way, and loved being able to send up her English, so-called 'betters'. She believed that all those in the British officer class were puffed up dummies, and having known quite a few 'Ruperts' I had, on the whole, to agree with her.

On another occasion she asked me if I could get the weekend off, and I managed to get one of the other lads to swap a couple of shifts with me.

I had no idea where we were going, and she directed me out into the country to a walled estate about forty kilometres from Celle.

As we were driving down the long, tree-lined avenue she told me we had been invited to the wedding of one of her friends, a millionaire's daughter, and we would be staying for the weekend.

My civilian clothes were of no more than mediocre quality, and I was immediately embarrassed and told her so.

She leant over and gave me one of those so wonderful kisses, making me weave all over the drive, and told me I was as good as any of the high society people we would be meeting.

Her mood had captured my imagination and I thought 'to hell with it – we won the war!' I parked the old Opel next to a Mercedes the size of a tank and looked around at the other vehicles, none of them worth less than the amount I made in ten years, many of them being polished yet again by their chauffeurs, who were looking down their noses at our carriage.

In that setting, my poor little car looked as incongruous as a down-and-out tramp among the glittering stars at a Hollywood awards ceremony.

Inside the huge mansion, we were introduced to everyone, including the Graf - his rank equivalent to an English Earl - and the Gräfin.

It was not that long after the war, and the attitudes of the German aristocracy were no different to those of the Hitler years.

Their expressions were deadpan, but I felt the inherent hostility.

The wedding and the reception were as one would expect in such an establishment, with dozens of servants doing everything necessary.

The day wore on, and though I would have liked to melt into the background, Gabrielle insisted on speaking to everyone, flaunting me, if you like, in a deliberate attempt to show them that she did not care for their opinions.

After a light late afternoon meal the Graf announced that the men would now go off to engage in some 'Schnepfen jagen'.

I was immediately intrigued. I had often hunted snipe in my youth - a wonderful quarry, since when they take off they fly straight for only a few yards, before jinking all over the sky.

The Graf barely hid a sneer as he stated, 'You do not hunt, of course, Friedrich, and can keep the ladies company.'

I was not having that!

I told him, 'Oh, yes, Edwin, I most certainly do. I have hunted all my life; every kind of quarry, including kudu, antelope and lions in Africa, and have often hunted Schnepfen at home.'

He was clearly astonished. 'Mit einer Flinte?'

Yes, I told him, but not the African game, of course, and possessed a twelve-gauge myself.

We had always walked them up, and I imagined that that is what we were about to do on the Graf's estate.

I could not have been more wrong.

He took me down to a room full of weapons, dozens of modern ones, shotguns and rifles, all by top manufacturers, including two pairs of Purdeys, which he showed me with pride.

On the walls there were also many antique weapons, a wonderful collection.

An ancient retainer rose from the bench where he had been sitting, working on the trigger mechanism of a shotgun, and bowed to his boss. He looked to be well over eighty years old, with skin the colour and texture of old, creased leather.

It transpired that he was the Graf's armourer – yes, the man actually had his own armourer! Unbelievable.

'Karl-Heinz,' he ordered, 'Fit Friedrich with a weapon.'

Fit me with a weapon? That was a first – I'd never been fitted for one before; hadn't a clue that it was necessary and just shot the gun as it was bought from the shop.

Karl-Heinz knew his job all right; he checked my eyesight, to determine which eye was dominant – something else I'd never even heard of at that time, though it became important later in life – measured my arm, handed me a shotgun he selected from one of the racks and had me bring it to the aim.

He moved around me, cocking his head to one side as he checked the position of my hands, had me aim at his eyes, moved the gun slightly on my shoulder, tut-tutted, as if he was blaming himself for a terrible error, then took the shotgun from me, lifted another from the same rack and had me repeat the exercise.

More checks, and then he nodded, satisfied, and I noticed the Graf smiling at his man's expertise, obviously pleased that he was showing this impecunious, benighted Englishman how thorough and efficient the Germans were, as if I was not already aware of that.

I had to admit that the weapon he gave me instantly felt part of me. I had learnt something very important from him and determined that when I got back home I would have my shotgun fitted for me.

The Graf pointed out that the gun I was holding was a Sauer and Son 'Meisterwerk' sidelock, as if that should mean something to me.

At the time I had no idea that it was anything special, but I have since done research on it and found that those shotguns were made especially to order, were terribly expensive and were considered heirlooms.

The guns in that room must have been worth tens of thousands of pounds, even at the prices of the time.

As we left that room, the old man surprised me greatly by winking at me conspiratorially behind the Graf's back.

Towards dusk, two shooting buses, full of Jäger-green-clad shooters, who had changed especially into their immaculate hunting attire, as per German tradition, to meet and intimidate their minute quarry, accompanied by one incorrectly dressed English pleb, drove some way from the mansion and up to a wood, which had a narrow track no more than fifteen feet wide running through it, resembling a fire-break.

I followed suit as they lined up along one side of it, with 'Weidmannsheil' and 'Weidmannsdank' being offered left, right, and centre, completely puzzled until the Graf, to my right, obviously there to keep an eye on me in case I decided to shoot one of his guests while I had the shotgun in my hands, told me that the Schnepfen would be driven off the marsh behind the wood by his men and would fly over us, at which time we would shoot at them.

It was an intriguing prospect, which could not possibly have been more sporting, and put the odds well in favour of the snipe.

The snipe has been recognised as the fastest migratory bird in the world, travelling as far as four thousand five hundred miles at speeds up to 97 kilometres an hour.

I didn't need to be a master mathematician to work out how much time those snipe were going to take to cross those fifteen feet above us. Let's be generous and say a second, though at top speed it would be only a fifth of that. Work out the odds!

I have, all my life, been one of those lucky people – a natural shot. I was never taught to shoot and didn't think anything about it until I left the RAF and joined two walk-up shoots, one run by a very good friend, and was soon banned from both of them because I shot everything while the rest were thinking about lifting their guns into the aim.

I can't remember when I first held a shotgun, but I do remember using a No.3 garden gun, a small shotgun, with cartridges much smaller than a .410, when I was six years old.

Back to cases: The snipe began to fly over, though not over me, their passing just audible as 'whooshes'. Two shots came from farther down the line; both misses.

I held the shotgun at the high port, hoping I was not offending protocol, since all the others had their guns pointing downwards in the gentlemanly 'waiting for driven pheasants' position, which gave them no chance whatsoever of raising the barrel to a firing position in time to shoot the snipe, and when one did at last appear in front of and over me I shot it, and it crumpled over the centre of the ride and fell in the wood behind me.

The Graf's dog, an eager Springer Spaniel, was on it immediately, picked it up delicately and took it back to its master.

I suddenly realised that there was a lot of noise – shouting from the troops – all shouts of congratulation.

The Graf was at my side, his hand extended.

'Mein lieber Mann! Das war unglaublich! Taü, taü, taü! Die erste seit '49. Ich gratuliere.'

I was suddenly his 'dear man', and what I had done was unbelievable.

I couldn't believe the fuss.

He shook my hand enthusiastically, the first to do so as they lined up to follow his lead.

Crappy old car and non-U clothes notwithstanding, I was the hero of the hour and nothing was too good for me.

At the time, it seemed a natural thing, but when I think back I realise that almost all of those men would have fought against us only a few years before and would no doubt have lost relatives during the conflict.

Their acceptance of me was a true indication of how sportsmanship can cross any barriers.

At the huge banquet that evening, the poor little snipe was first carried around the table on a silver platter in a march of honour and then placed as a centrepiece on top of it.

At the end of the meal, speeches were made by the groom, the best man and the bride's father regarding the nuptials, and at the end the Graf's peroration was to again congratulate Yours Truly on the tremendous achievement. He pointed once more at the pitiful little corpse.

The following day he made a point of taking me round the whole estate, showing off his pheasant poults and telling me that I would be receiving an invitation to each of his shoots. There were also duck on his three carefully dug splashes, and, he said, if I was interested in deer stalking he could lend me a rifle.

I must admit I was highly flattered and thanked him, intending to take full advantage of his offers.

We left during the afternoon, and Gabrielle pretended a yawn. In that wonderfully clever, overdone, upper-class English she was so good at she pronounced, 'Terribly boring people, what?'

We both fell about laughing, which is not the way to drive an Opel P4, or any other car for that matter. Luckily, there was no other traffic.

She had her list of things on an importance rating, however, and murmured, 'Lovely bed though.'

Those millionaire friends of hers were the only Germans I had met that I had not asked a particular question. I think, if I had, I might have been shot as fair game.

An avid reader all my life, I had, some months before, read a book by a Hungarian guy called George Mikes, pronounced Gee-org Meekesh, entitled, '*How to be an Alien*'. In it he refers to an eighteen-month period he spent in Germany after the war, trying to find a Nazi.

After questioning scores of people, he at last found one old man who grudgingly admitted that yes, he had been a member of the Nazi party. He had joined, he said, when he was so blind drunk one night in a Munich Bierkeller in 1933 that he did not know what he was doing, but had resigned from the party immediately the next morning when he was sober again and realised with horror what he had done.

Like George Mikes, I had tried that question on most of the Germans I got to know, and the almost terrified looks I received from a great many of them while they looked over their shoulders and all around them to see if anyone had heard me ask the question belied the universal whispered answer, 'No, absolutely not.' Quite often there was an additional comment, like, 'I hated what they were doing.' And this, remember, was *ten years* after the end of the war!

Though hidden, there remained a real Nazi presence, and the populace was still scared witless of the members. Most of them knew which of their neighbours and acquaintances to be afraid of too!

The only one who answered me in the positive was Gabrielle.

She had shrugged and laughed, 'Of course, Friedrich. Everyone was.'

To my additional question, 'Were you in the Gestapo?' she had, after a slight hesitation, merely cocked her head to one side, lifted an eyebrow, pursed those wonderful lips and looked into my eyes, with the hint of a smile in her own.

I had the distinct impression that she had been, since with her impeccable English and inherent intelligence she would have been a tremendous asset to them, and talent like that in a desperate war situation would certainly not have been wasted.

I decided it was better not to pursue the matter. I might have learnt something I did not like.

Whatever else she might have been, she was a survivor, and one thing was for sure: with her figure, she would have made a damned fine replacement for Helga in *'Allo, 'Allo.* I could clearly imagine her standing there proudly in that black underwear with a whip in her hand. She would be capable of anything.

When I asked her those questions I was only six weeks from the end of my tour and I did what everyone else in the Code and Cypher section had done and applied for an extension, expecting it to be rubber-stamped, as all the others had been, since we were so short of trained staff.

To my horror it was turned down, and I couldn't believe it.

I asked to see the Adjutant.

'There must be some mistake, sir. You know how low on manpower we are.'

'No mistake, Nash.' He said, 'You're on your way.'

'But, sir. You need me. My work is perfectly good, as you know.'

'Yes, I do know, and yes, we do need you, quite badly in fact, but man, have you looked in a mirror recently? You're what? Twenty-three? You look sixty-three. I know why too.'

His voice lowered, and in a tone that made him sound more like an old friend who felt sorry for me, he advised, 'Look, go home and take a month or two to recuperate, and then you can come back and carry on from where you left off. You know you can apply for overseas again the moment you reach your new unit, and you could be back here in six months. She might wait for you.'

He sounded doubtful, and, as it turned out, with good reason.

I protested, but in vain.

Looking back, I know he did me a huge favour, even though it felt like a death sentence at the time.

He was right about my looks. For months I had been subsisting on about four hours' sleep a day, and if Gabrielle was in bed with me during those four hours there was not much sleeping done. I did look rough, but I was distraught.

I was sure I loved her and wanted to marry her, forgetting my girlfriend back in Blighty altogether. I hadn't even written to her for three months, though her letters arrived regularly every second day.

When I told Gabrielle the news and asked her to come back to England and marry me she said that it was impossible, but of course she would wait for me and would write every day.

We made every minute count during the time we had left; so much so that I looked more like seventy than sixty-three!

Before leaving, I made a gift of the old Opel to Ken.

When my posting came through I could not believe it: I was posted to RAF Scampton, in charge of the telephone exchange. Out of the 'Y' Service.

Someone had clanged!

I spent my disembarkation leave moping. Every day I wrote a long, loving letter to Gabrielle, expressing my love in every way possible, including bad poetry, and the letters began arriving from her, each one with a large lipstick imprint of her generous lips on the stuck-down flap, which caused my mother to growl with disgust each time she handed me one of them while I was on leave, her disgust mainly due to the way I had treated Jacquie, my girlfriend, whom I hadn't yet bothered to go and see, remaining in the house all the time.

I wrote to Ken too, telling him how much I missed Gabrielle and my intention of returning to marry her.

I reported to Scampton two days early, glad to get away from home.

The job, I found, had me in charge of a large telephone exchange, with a staff of twenty-two WAAFs, working shifts.

Most men in that position would have said a few Hail Marys in thanks, but I was still too full of Gabrielle.

The girls were unaware of that, of course, and set about 'welcoming' me in their own fashion.

Cries of, 'Oh, this hole just isn't big enough – I can't get it in', 'I'm having trouble with this jack', 'It's stuck in now', 'My God! I can't get it out!' and many similar expressions kept me grinning like an idiot, my face averted, trying not to show it.

It was a game and helped to while away a lot of boring hours.

Nowadays, I guess, it would be called 'sexual harassment', but it was all good natured tom-foolery and I took it as it was meant.

I think after a couple of weeks my staff must have thought I was gay, because I turned down a couple of thinly veiled offers from beautiful girls and was a bit of an old grouch.

At least, my time there gave me another skill: I learnt everything there was to know about a PBX, and could work a position as well as any of the girls.

The first thing I'd done on reaching the camp was to apply for overseas, and I kept hoping, but nothing came of it.

The letters from Gabrielle dwindled to a stop, and I was going out of my mind with frustrated love until I received a letter from Ken, in which he urged me to forget her.

'Her ex-husband moved in with her the day after you left', he wrote, 'and he's still living with her.'

It hurt like hell, but it enabled the start of my recuperation.

Though the job in the telephone exchange was a walk in the park, I missed the work I had been doing in the intercept trade, and one day, in desperation, I rode to 399 Signals Unit, Digby, just down the road from Scampton, on the Triumph 500 I'd bought on leave before going to Scampton, and at the Signals Unit guardroom asked to speak to the Officer in charge.

For once, I found an intelligent 'snowdrop' on duty, and he rang through and passed on my request.

An elderly Flight Lieutenant I didn't recognise came to the gate just a few minutes later and walked out into the sun to speak to me.

I gave him my history, including the fact that I was Top Secret Codeword cleared, and told him the current problem.

'You'd like to come back into the Organisation?'

'Yes, sir.'

'Very well. Leave it with me. I'll see what I can do.'

He was as good as his word, and six weeks after arriving at Scampton I was posted to Diggers.

There were actually real tears and hugs from some of my short-lived staff.

I couldn't have been that bad a boss.

CHAPTER FOUR

Digby, whose station motto is *'Icarus Renatus' – (Icarus Reborn), is a most interesting station. Originally called RAF Scopwick, it is the very oldest station in the RAF, dating from 1918, having been set up originally as a Royal Naval Air Station in 1914, and a list of its commanding officers reads like the Who's Who of the RAF, including, on its becoming No 3 Flying Training School in April 1920, Squadron Leader AT Harris, who during the Second World War was so well known as Air Marshall 'Bomber' Harris GCB OBE AFC; Wing Commander Tedder, later to become Lord Tedder and an Air Marshall with the GCB; Group Captain Leigh Mallory, later Marshall of the RAF KCB DSO and bar, and a real 'character' - Wing Commander Sidney 'Crasher' Smith DSO DFC, renowned for his undercarriage-bashing landings, which were due to an eye defect. On one memorable day he managed to crunch three aircraft. The Germans could have used him as a secret weapon!

During the Second World War when it was an operational flying station both Guy Gibson and Douglas Bader were stationed and flew from there.

A Roll of Honour indeed.

Going from the sublime to the Gorblimey, Yours Truly, an infinitely less famous serviceman, found himself to be a set-room wallah again, this time as a deputy supervisor.

The sets – about thirty of them spread out along the opposite sides of the long walls – were manned on a roughly fifty-fifty basis by RAF personnel and civilian operators, and the two supervisors were a civilian and either a Flight Sergeant or a Warrant Officer.

The work was comparatively easy, and left me plenty of time to think of other things.

I'd noticed dozens of rabbits running about and feeding on the airfield/aerial farm, where there were lots of mounds over shelters and storage units, none of which were any longer in use. My poacher's eye had also noted the dozens of pheasants that flew up the trees bordering the airfield as it became dusk every day.

Sleaford, the nearest town, was sleepy, with little in the way of entertainment, except the occasional dance, and my inclination always, even now, to get at least forty-eight hours out of every twenty-four, had me looking for other things than work to keep my interest going.

I bought a shotgun and applied for permission to shoot on the camp grounds. Those rabbits, which had never had it so good, were about to get a nasty surprise.

I had to see the Adjutant, who asked about my shooting history. I told him I'd been using a shotgun since I was knee-high to a duck, and that analogy got me the necessary permission.

'But,' he warned, 'the pheasants are off-limits. We have very good relations with our neighbours, the Lincolnshire Crop Dryers' Association, and I need you to be very careful not to upset them.'

I was happy with that at the time and assured him that I would not touch the 'long-tailed-uns'. (Well, not unless one committed suicide in front of me.) The main consideration was that I would not be able to cook them, living in the barrack block as I did.

As I left his office a corporal I did not know came after me and asked, 'Can I have a quiet word?'

He introduced himself as Gerry Jermy and told me he worked in the SWO's office and was living with his wife in married quarters. His accent was pure Norfolk, and I recognised a soul-mate.

He was, even on first sight, a rough diamond; chunkily built, with a sun-tanned, heavily lined face and a forthright manner.

I liked him immediately. He was my kind of man.

'Did you get permission?' He asked, and I told him I had.

'Jammy sod!' He exclaimed, 'I applied and was turned down.'

That got me thinking.

'What if I put in another application – to run a Gun Club?'

'Do you think they'll wear it?'

I shrugged, 'If yew dun't ask...'

He continued the old Norfolk expression: ...yew dun't want. And if yew do ask...'

He let me finish, 'Yew dun't git.'

We both laughed.

'I'll do it. Have you got a Gen App?'

He led me into the SWO's office, which was empty and found me a form, which I filled in on the spot.

He asked, 'How are you going to tackle the rabbits?'

I'd been giving it a lot of thought, 'Without a ferret I was going to lie up and wait for them to come out of their burrows, but the only trouble with that is that I'd probably only get a couple of shots, and the rest would stay below.'

His mind was following the same lines as my own, 'Why don't you get a ferret?'

'I'd like to, but where could I keep it?'

He grinned, and his grin was wicked, 'My back garden.'

'Won't your wife mind?'

The grin widened, 'You must be joking.'

He had old-fashioned ideas about the place of women, and that marriage, which did not last long, was only the first of three. The first two were, as he put it, 'disasters', and the third and longest a magnificent success.

The upshot was that we bought two ferrets, a Joey and a Jill, intending to breed them and sell the offspring, which we did with great success. They were rampant little devils.

The Gun Club was authorised, and I was given the key to a cellar, where there were half a dozen .22 rifles locked in a rack, and a 25-yard range, unused for quite a number of years.

I had to sign for everything and keep the register of ammunition used, supplied free by the RAF, and the accounts, but that was no problem.

I had told the Adjutant that the Club would be open to anyone who wished to join, but apart from running a token target shoot once a fortnight, when the odd airman or NCO would turn up, Gerry and I were the only real members.

We bought nets and had a field day with the rabbits, netting every hole but two – one for each of us to shoot at the rabbits that bolted.

Those that were caught in the nets were dispatched and added to the pile of prey.

There was no lack of buyers for them, and we were soon supplying the Officers' and Sergeants' messes, as well as the individual officers, NCOs and civilian ops on a regular basis.

One evening, as we set the nets under a beautiful cloudless sky, we saw an individual in baggy plus-fours and country tweed jacket striding across the aerial farm towards us.

It didn't worry us, since what we were doing was totally legitimate – an unusual situation for both of us – Gerry, like me, having poached throughout most of his youth!

The stranger came up to us, glanced admiringly at the large pile of dead rabbits, and introduced himself as William Blake, the Head Gamekeeper for the Crop Growers Association.

He'd heard the shooting and was interested to know what was going on and who was involved. We knew his real intention was to find out if his pheasants were at risk.

He seemed a decent enough guy; heavily built, with a chunky, weather-beaten face and a no-nonsense manner.

We told him our story and were surprised when he asked, 'Do you do any pigeon shooting?'

Gerry and I looked at each other. Was there water at the bottom of a well?

'We do!' We said together.

He'd obviously sized us up and found us not wanting, because he then told us, 'We grow four thousand acres of peas and we are plagued with pigeons that have come over from Norway, as they do every year. They are completely uneducated, because they've never been shot at, not like the English ones. My lads and I can't cope with them. If you'd like to help us you'll get free cartridges and a packed lunch.'

He gave us directions and we told him what days we were free.

His statement about the pigeons being uneducated, though we had doubted it at the time, was absolutely true.

The ones we were used to shooting would disappear over the far horizon after one shot. Those Norwegian ones would come in as a cloud of fifty or sixty at a time, and we'd drop two each. They would then fly around in a circle and come back in again, to lose another four from the flock. That would happen all day long, while others joined them.

The barrels became too hot to hold. It was some of the most fabulous pigeon sport I have ever enjoyed, and that is saying something, since I have been very lucky in having pigeon shooting available wherever I've been. Often, after leaving the RAF, I had 200-plus pigeon days in winter, shooting over rape, but that time in Lincolnshire was nothing short of a pigeon shooter's Mecca.

Best of all, it cost us nothing. Blake gave us four hundred cartridges each at the start of the day and came around again at lunchtime with a top quality packed lunch and gave us four hundred more each. And he did not want any of the birds or any unused cartridges back – additional bonuses.

Pigeon was added to the menu in the messes and homes of the officers, civilians and other ranks, and we had to sell birds regularly to a game dealer in Sleaford - we had so many.

It was not all play, of course. The intercept business was my main one, and at work in the pleasantly airy, well lit set room, my main job was as a trouble shooter.

If a set went wrong I called the technician and for continuity of intercept arranged for the operator to move to one of the two spare positions, which were kept for that purpose, and if one of the lads wanted to go to the toilet, I sat on his set while he went, keeping my hand in with the Morse and getting experience of a large number of Russian nets. I did not have too many minutes free during any shift, but those that I did have were used to good effect.

Many of the civilian operators and some of the RAF personnel were heavily into horse racing, and I became interested, because one of the civilians had a brother who worked at a racing stable up north and gave us tips, which almost always produced a winner.

It seemed like easy money and was, using his tips, but I began to study form and found that 2-year olds seemed to be the most consistent of all the horses running.

It made sense, since, as they were little more than babies, they were full of energy, had learnt no bad habits like older horses and ran their hearts out every time, unless they were ill.

A more important factor was that although it was a fact of life that some trainers often deliberately ran older horses in races they could not possibly win, by entering them for a race whose distance they were not effective over, or on a left or right hand track, when they knew the horse was only effective on the other, or gave the jockey instructions to hold them back, in order to have improved odds in later races, they had a vested interest in making sure that their two-year-olds ran to the best of their ability, so that they could get the best prices for them when they sold them on as three-year-olds.

The *Racing Post*, I found out, gave speed figures for every horse in every race run, based on the actual speed achieved compared with standard time for the course and distance.

The figure was then adjusted, by taking into consideration the jockey weight carried during that particular race, so that the *Racing Post* figure was what the horse would have achieved had it been carrying nine stone exactly, one pound in weight being judged as one point. The speed figures for the horses that followed the winner home were reckoned out by deducting three points for each full horse length, two for half a length and one for a head. A figure of 100 was used as par for the average horse.

I began to write down the name of each two-year-old that ran, with its speed figure for each race in which it took part next to it, in a notebook with alphabetical sections. For the first three months of the season they ran only over five furlongs, so that was not an issue, and in those days, two-year-olds did not begin their careers until the first of March.

Then I started to work out the two-year-old races for each day, adjusting the *Post's* figures according to the weight that each horse would carry in that race.

It soon emerged that most of the horses were highly consistent in their speed figures for consecutive races, most of them hardly changing at all or improving slightly, and that my system would give me around seventy percent winners.

The going had an effect, but rarely in summer was it heavy, or even soft, so it was not often a factor to be reckoned with.

I was obviously not the only punter doing something similar, because the starting prices reflected the ability of the runners, and the best horses according to my figures were generally odds-on, instead of odds-against.

To make serious money with those prices one would have needed to stake in hundreds if staking on individual horses, and I didn't have that sort of money, so I began to do 'Yankees' – a betting system which covers four horses with eleven bets - six doubles, four trebles and an accumulator.

My one stipulation was that any horse I backed should, on my figures, be clear of the others in its race by at least three points – a horse length.

It was incredibly accurate, and I was getting four out of four at least three times a week. Betting only in shillings, one shilling for each bet, I was getting back twenty or thirty times my stake money each week.

On the first of May, the two-year olds began to race over six furlongs, and that made quite a difference, since some were better over that distance and some were not.

I altered my system of recording, using red pen for the six furlong races.

By this time I was giving all the racing men on the unit horses to back.

They were, to start with, dubious, but one race convinced them all.

The favourite, a horse called *Brown Mug*, was one with a speed rating that was up there with the best – 120. (The highest I ever came across was 138, and that horse won the Derby the following year.)

*Brown Mug's* forecast SP – starting price – was ten to one on, meaning that one had to stake ten shillings on the horse to win one, indicating that the bookies took it to be a nailed-on certainty.

It was carrying nine stone ten pounds, and by deducting the ten points for the ten extra pounds it was carrying its rating for the race worked out at 110.

The rest of the runners, except one, which had not yet won a race or been placed, did not come close to that figure, but that one, the biggest outsider in the race at a forecast starting price of 33 to 1, had the lowly speed figure of 69 and was carrying the lowest weight – just seven stone ten pounds, three stones less than the favourite. With the allowance of 42 pounds the adjustment brought its figure for that race to 111 – one point clear of the favourite.

It's name was *Star Combine*.

It did not have the necessary three points clear that I used as my criterion to back a horse, and I was going to leave it out of my bets for the day, but I then heard an announcement that Brown Mug had been withdrawn from the race, so included it in my Yankee selections and gave them to my civilian and RAF friends.

One of the staff usually listened to the races on a little radio, and an hour before *Star Combine's* race heard an announcement that *Brown Mug* had been put back into the race.

I was damned annoyed. Yes, my little outsider did have a point in hand over the favourite, but the favourite had not been hard pressed in any of his three races, and I knew from experience that a good horse can always pull a bit extra out of the bag when under pressure.

It would be a close thing, but I guessed my selection would just lose out.

I put a brave face on it though and told the punters that it should win, keeping my fingers firmly crossed.

Four of us managed to listen to the race, and it was one of the most nail-biting finishes I have ever experienced.

Star Combine was in front by three lengths at the one furlong marker and Brown Mug was making up ground as they sped towards the finishing line.

Brown Mug got his head in front forty yards from the post, but then Star Combine fought back – and won by a nose.

My selections were never queried after that.

The system only worked from the first of May to the first of August, when the trainers started to race their two-year-olds over seven furlongs and a mile, and took up around forty hours a week, recording and working out speed figures, but it was phenomenally accurate for those three months, and in the three years that I worked it my average profit was 1500 points.

An interesting result was that I was banned by two of the local bookmakers and had to have someone else place my bets for me. They only wanted losers, and were not happy bunnies when a punter won so regularly – particularly someone who was successful with Yankees.

One morning, for some reason I have never been able to understand, I was offered, with five other NCOs, a chance to make a one-day visit to the SIGINT site at RAF Chicksands, which had been in operation for a very long time, and had, during the Second World War, intercepted German radio traffic. At the site, alongside the RAF contingent, there were members of the American 6950th Electronic Security Group doing the same job.

The main reason for our visit was to see in the flesh, as it were, the huge AN/FLR-9 Wüllenweber antenna array, which was close to 1500 feet in diameter, and which formed part of the *Iron Horse* HF D/F network.

We had seen pictures of it, of course, and read about it, but one had to physically look at it to really appreciate its fantastic size.

Maybe they just wanted to impress us.

Now all that is left of that wonderful array are the concrete base blocks, looking for all the world like some latter-day, flattened Stonehenge.

The unit, however, continues in existence and now houses DISC – The Defence, Intelligence and Security Centre and is also the Headquarters of the Intelligence Corps. It conducts the training for all three of the British Forces, as well as the members of the Civil Service.

It was a visit I am glad I made, as it helped to complete the picture of the service I had given a big part of my life to.

CHAPTER FIVE

I had been going back to Norfolk quite often at weekends and had made it up with Jacquie, having admitted to the affair with Gabrielle, though with no details, of course. We'd become engaged.

In April, out of the blue, I was seconded back to Compton to do the Teleg I course, which I found very easy, and was surprised to then be sent to Bletchley Park for another fairly lengthy advanced course, leading to the Civil Service civilian operators' PQL qualification.

There I met up with another corporal who was to become my best friend, and with whom I am still in daily touch by email, Chris Boyd, who has recently published his own memoirs of his time in the 'Y' Service – *'Special Operator'*. Neither of us knew at the time what job we were destined for or where, but we knew we would be working together with another corporal, whom I shall call 'the Third Man', for reasons that will become clear later.

The accommodation was in the Manor itself, and the excellent meals we enjoyed were dished up in the very civilised dining room just inside the main gate.

At the time I had not the slightest idea that I and the two others had already been earmarked for a specialist job in Berlin, though in retrospect I believe it to have been so. That job would be to replace three civilians, and in order, I imagine, not to upset the civilian operators' union, which was quite strong and voluble, we were required to show that we were as competent as they were, and in order to demonstrate that we had to pass the stringent PQL test.

To do that we were given practice each day with a class of civilians, which included a lot of Morse, slip reading, and listening to and logging what sounded like real intercepts, but which could have been synthesised, many of them being extremely weak and with a lot of interference of one kind and another, before taking the test, which was fifteen minutes of continuous Morse, consisting of five minutes of plain language, five minutes of figure groups and five minutes of mixed letters and figures, all at 25 words per minute.

The 'P' stood for the ability to receive at that speed for that length of time; the 'Q' indicated a result with less than eight errors overall, and the 'L' was for legibility. Having copied everything in the 15 minutes it had to be perfectly readable and well written.

All three of us passed it with flying colours and returned to our units.

Wanting to see more of the world, I had applied several times for an overseas posting, and at last one came up, and an unusual one at that, but it had nothing to do with my applications.

Someone Up There knew long before we did what we were destined for.

The posting date was a couple of months away and Jacquie and I decided that we should get married before I went abroad.

Her mother was dead set against the marriage, but we did it anyway, in June 1955. The weather was great and everything went off well.

Money being tight, the honeymoon was merely a weekend in a hotel at East Runton, which I remember mostly for the evening meal on the Saturday, when, trying to shovel the lead-shot-like peas onto my fork, I had sent a whole shower of them flying through the air across the room and watched them bounce under the legs of the other diners.

Every eye in the room turned towards me in disapproval.

The embarrassment was awful, but Jacquie was having a hell of a job not to laugh.

Nowadays, of course, I would call the waiter over and complain about the state of the peas, (and the rest of that truly dreadful meal), but, young as I was and out of my comfort zone, I felt to blame.

It was not a memorable honeymoon, since the excitement had brought on Jacquie's period a fortnight early. Ah, well, we had the whole of the future.

I, Chris, and the Third Man had been told that our posting was to RAF Gatow, in Berlin, but that is not where we were sent.

Off we went on the boat train and arrived at Goch, on the Dutch border on the 16th October 1955, staying in transit there for just one day before moving on to 646 Signals Unit, Scharfoldendorf, which had previously been 291SU.

It sat high in the mountains about sixty kilometres south of Hannover in Niedersachsen – Lower Saxony - a most interesting place, since, sited as it was on the ridge of the Ith Hills, one of the buildings - the old German Schloss - the castle – whose former splendour was entirely absent, since it was now home to the mess, could be seen for miles.

The Unit had its own extra-large motor transport section, a NAAFI, a signals block, top quality living accommodation and even a swimming pool, and had been titled 646 SU from about October of 1952, having been spawned from what had originally and euphemistically been called an Air Scientific Research Unit, based at Obenkirchen.

That was an entirely mobile unit, whose vehicles were sent out from the base to sites near the border to intercept Russian and East German transmissions.

The mobile tradition remained, though as only a part of the operations of the Unit.

646 had three listening post outstations: Putlos, northeast of Hamburg, Gifthorn, on Luneburg Heath, about 35 kilometres northeast of Hannover, and Gatow, in Berlin, named 3 Detachment, where in the future I would spend seven years of my service.

Of all the units based in Germany, it had the only motto in German – *'Kein Hindernis zu Hoch'*, courtesy of the efforts of Wing Commander Eric Ackerman, GM, the commanding officer - a highly intelligent man and, strangely, a civilian, who held an honorary commission.

His George Medal had been awarded for his many flights over Germany during the war, investigating German radars at first hand, at tremendous risk to his personal safety.

The nearest village, at the foot of the hill, was Eschershausen, where we very quickly discovered the Café Bremer, a home from home for many of the airmen from the unit. The only problem with using that favourite watering hole was the long and wearisome trek back uphill through the pine woods, often in the rain, but we were stoic and stood it.

Chris, the Third Man and I, for some reason, had not been expected and were in a kind of limbo, not being employed on intercept duties, but we did have time to attend the weekly dances in the mess, to which the nurses from the Höxter hospital, and also the local girls were invited. There were always plenty of attractive female partners to dance with, and I had a further chance to improve my German.

One thing I do recall quite clearly was Chris, having spent the whole of one such evening with one girl, wanted to walk her home at the end of the dance.

He at that time did not speak German, but asked me if I could help him.

I implored her to allow him to walk her home – she lived quite a way the other side of Eschershausen - and she seemed inclined to agree, but wanted to know more about him before allowing him to do so. During the course of the evening we had downed quite a few drinks, as you do, and with alcohol-fuelled enthusiasm and not too much common sense I decided I would try to impress her.

I Introduced him as 'Furst Kristophe von Bolen und Halbach und Kapellenhagen', using the family title of George Krupp of German heavy industry fame, with the added name of one of the tiny local villages, and basically imbuing him with a rank equivalent to a prince and a parentage that would place him at the top of German aristocracy.

Oh, yes, it was bloody ridiculous, but just imagine the booze-influenced scene.

I don't know how much of it she believed – I guess thinking back probably none of it - but he did get to accompany her home, and had a tiring, long walk back through the damp, dripping fir woods for his trouble. We have often chuckled about that little episode.

I, of course, as a newly married man, could inspect and enjoy dancing with the delights, but was not permitted to inhale.

Because those who ran the unit did not know what to do with us, and since I was a qualified service driver, one day I found myself at the wheel of one of the three-and-a-half-ton Magirus Deutz RVs – radio vehicles – heading to a location several hours away and much nearer to the border of East Germany, where we erected the directional aerials attached to the roof and spent a couple of days listening to selected Russian air force units on exercise. Their signals were five by nine, much better than they were at Scharf.

One of the other lads on that little jaunt told me that such trips were often carried out by the unit, and that in the winter they regularly had trouble starting the trucks when they wanted to go home, because the diesel had frozen in the tanks. The electric heaters, tubes about eighteen inches long, with many large fins to give off heat, which were used to warm the minute set room in the back of the RV, also often failed to work, probably because of transformer troubles.

One of those heaters quite miraculously came into my possession and I somehow got it back home. It still resides in my garage at the bottom of my garden, and I have occasionally used it when I've been working there in the winter. It might not have worked in the RV, but it has never let me down at home.

I believe that there were so many RVs at Scharf because it was intended that in the event of an invasion by the Russians – seen as highly possible at that time - the unit could become mobile, move west and continue monitoring the nets they were responsible for. The frequent exercises using the vehicles not only kept them operational but gave many of the staff the practice they would need if it ever came to a shooting war.

One very wet day, the 29th October 1955, when we had begun to think we would be in occupational limbo for ever, we were told to get our gear together – we were going back to Blighty for what was referred to as a 'briefing' at GCHQ.

After another trip on the boat train and British railways we arrived at RAF Innsworth, where we were billeted for the short duration of our stay, although for some incomprehensible reason we were officially on the strength of AMU Ruislip.

Misplaced secrecy? It's possible.

At GCHQ we were informed that we would be replacing three civilians in Berlin, and though it was not said out loud, we were given the distinct impression that the reason was a definite lack of product. Our job, an exciting prospect, would be to search the airwaves for the transmissions of East German and Russian secret agents active in the West, and we were allowed to hear several recordings of such transmissions, so that we would know what to listen for.

The job entailed sitting in front of a pair of receivers, turning the dial of the right hand one continuously throughout our watch, looking for a control station transmission, which alerted us to an impending reply from an agent. Very occasionally, we would find an outstation first.

The agent would wait at the appointed time for a signal from the control station, situated either in East Berlin or Moscow, which would transmit a three-figure callsign about five or six times, and the agent, using a suitcase transmitter, would come up in answer on an entirely different frequency, probably as much as two Megaherz distant from that of the control station, answering with just two or three transmissions of his callsign, and then there would follow a burst transmission.

We were told that our job would be to continually search the whole frequency range that they used – around five megacycles - for the control station, which never used the same frequency twice, and having found the control, frantically search the ether, turning the dial of the other receiver constantly, for the outstation. Then, having found it, slam the Ferrograph recorder on to record the burst transmission, while using something like the toes of the left foot to grip the telephone and call up the direction finding station to get them to take a bearing. If they could have trained an octopus for the job it would have been more efficient.

Since the agent transmission rarely lasted more than half a minute, it is easy to understand why not many transmissions were DFed.

It sounded like an intriguing and highly demanding job, and was, we found.

We finally arrived at Gatow on the 9th November 1955, having by-passed Scharfoldendorf this time.

The monitoring station was on the second floor of Station Headquarters, and our little room was attainable via the stairs through a small gate guarded by an RAF Regiment guy armed with a Sten gun - always loaded. Along the corridor were the Linguists, both RAF and Intelligence Corps, the latter for some reason disguised as members of the Royal Signals, though I am sure that did not fool the Russians for one instant.

That was to be our home for a year, before we moved to Hanbury Block.

We located the room all right, but there was no sign of the civilian operators.

What we did find were log pads completed for the next three days, all filled out in neat handwriting with '*NIL REQUIRED HEARD*'.

It was no wonder the civilians were being replaced.

We discovered that they had code names that were the positions on a cricket field, like 'Shortstop' and 'Long Leg', and that the signals they sent back to GCHQ were addressed to the 'Pavilion'.

If they were trying to fool anyone intercepting their signals with that, it was a pretty puerile effort.

We began work immediately after having handed in our completed blue chits, the writing of the dentist's signature on mine bearing a strangely close resemblance to my own. The poor man must have been getting cramps in his writing hand, because on Chris' chit the script was entirely different.

The Third Man, of course, not willing to live in the least dangerously, had obtained a genuine John Hancock.

Looking at the requirements of the job, we decided on a watch system, which had two of us working the days and one the nights.

It was three days before we located one of the civilian operators we were replacing.

He was playing snooker in the sergeants' mess!

He rang the others in a panic, and we met up with them - three totally devastated guys, who could not comprehend, or indeed believe, their instant, unexpected expulsion, two of them almost in tears, because they had recently bought cars on the export list and had not had them the requisite twelve months to avoid customs duty if imported back into England. The thought of losing their overseas allowances, which were much greater than ours, was another severe blow.

Frantic signals were sent off, both to GCHQ and to their union headquarters, and answers received before they finally believed their fate.

They assured us that intercepts were extremely rare – almost non-existent, in fact, and almost begged us not to over-exert ourselves in searching for them.

They knew they had been found out and that the writing was on the wall.

I personally thought that they'd had a damned raw deal in not having been warned, despite the fact that they had brought it on themselves.

To be removed from the crease without the slightest forewarning from the Pavilion was not really cricket, if I might be allowed to use their own terminology.

We had our first intercept on the second day, a control station so loud that it seemed to be in the same room, three figures repeated, and started the search for the agent, but no luck on that occasion. At least, we knew the job was a live one.

At that time, we were still using the HRO receiver we were so well used to.

It was to be almost a month before one of us found an answering agent and managed to record the burst, but after that our rapidly increasing expertise enabled us to regularly intercept them, usually four or five times a week.

We recorded the burst at the top speed of the Ferrograph, a wonderfully robust and efficient machine, then played it back at the slowest speed and re-recorded it on a second Ferrograph at top speed before playing it back once more, again at the slowest speed.

The burst transmission was sent at approximately 400 words per minute, and slowing it down twice brought it down to about 25. We were then able to transcribe it onto message logs. They went off to 'Q' by courier, along with the recordings.

Chris and I found a couple of watering holes we liked very much: *Der dicke Heinrich*, in Keithstrasse, frequented by many of our fellow airmen from Gatow, and the tiny *Zum Dorfkrug* in Kladow, just behind the camp.

The owner of the latter, a dark haired, thirty-something, good looking woman called Liese, was another who helped me with my German, and I spent hours talking to her while sinking a couple of Schultheiss, which for years afterwards I hankered for but couldn't get and can now buy from the local Aldi store, to the detriment of my belly.

Though there were married quarters on the base, there were not enough, and if I wanted my wife with me I would have to find civilian accommodation, which was also short.

I put out feelers in many directions and after a couple of days was told by a friend about a summerhouse in a German woman's garden that she was willing to rent out. It was in the Krampnitzer Weg, Kladow, behind the airfield and about two miles from the main gate.

Frau Henke, the owner, was, she told me, seventy-four, and had been married to an important aristocrat with a large estate before the Russians made her flee from her home in the East. Looking at her, I took her assertions with a great pinch of salt.

She looked and sounded like a typical 'Kartoffelfrau', and I guessed the nearest she had ever got to an aristocrat was as one of his maids.

She was, and never had been, a beauty. Fat and overflowing, with a moon face, disfigured by a large wart on one side of her nose, and another on her wispy, bearded chin, she was the epitome of a money-grabbing landlady, but her summerhouse was the only game in town, and I was pretty desperate.

Looking at it on a gorgeously sunny autumn afternoon, with a temperature in the high twenties, it looked okay, although it was very small.

The only thing to cook on was a one-ring gas burner, which would make anything other than very simple meals impossible, and there was no heating, but on a day like that one takes no notice of such minor problems.

I applied for the place to be taken on as private accommodation, and after a bit of vetting it was approved, and I sent for Jacquie, who came out the following week.

During that week, chatting to one of the German clerks who worked in SHQ, Heinrich, a member of the GSO, the German Services Organisation, whose members carried out all sorts of duties from clerical work to gardening, I found that he was a qualified teacher and asked if he would be prepared to check translations for me for a packet of fags a time.

He agreed, and for the first one I picked a most difficult passage from a book I was reading. It included the description of a grand old house, and one sentence included the phrase 'shingle tortured mansards'. I translated it as 'kieselgefolterte Mansarden'.

He protested, 'You can't say that. It doesn't exist.'

I laughed and pointed out, 'It doesn't exist in English either.' But I resolved to stick to straightforward, simple prose after that, and he helped me considerably over the next few months.

I met Jacquie when she landed at Templehof and we moved in.

At last we had a proper honeymoon, and made good use of it.

Frau Henke became a bit of a problem. She was obviously lonely, and kept turning up at the door of the summerhouse on all sorts of pretexts, wanting to talk.

It was not so bad when I was present, but Jacquie had not a word of German, and the old lady not a word of English, so communication was almost impossible.

As autumn rolled into winter we found that cramming on more and more clothing was not enough to keep us warm.

I bought a gas heater from the main NAAFI, situated in Summit House, on Theodor Heuss Platz, previously called Adolf Hitler Platz, which helped, but solving one problem created another: for every pint of gas burnt a pint of water was produced, which made the furniture and our clothing stored in the cupboard and drawers damp.

It was a typical Berlin winter, with the wind coming directly from Siberia, giving temperatures of twenty below.

We shook with cold, and had thick icicles on the insides of the windows.

One day a couple of good friends, Geoff, and his wife, Dora, visited.

They took one look, appalled, exchanged glances and insisted, 'You can't live here! You're moving in with us.'

They would not take no for an answer.

The sharing of quarters was in some cases allowed, providing there was enough accommodation for the two families. Geoff and Dora had just one little boy and there were three bedrooms in the quarter, so no problem.

Permission was granted and we moved out of our igloo and into the luxury of a centrally heated flat. Frau Henke was not best pleased.

We got on well, sharing the cooking and housework.

Miraculously, after only a month sharing, I was given a quarter – a flat over the airman's mess, and we moved in. Jacquie was two months pregnant.

At last I had time for other things and I purchased a car, a second-hand maroon Standard Vanguard, unusual in that it had a column gear shift and only three forward gears, but they were all synchromesh, and it was fitted with a Laycock de Normanville overdrive, giving it in effect five gears. The top speed was a phenomenal 78mph!

With its sloping back it reminded one of the pre-war American Plymouth, but the Russians reckoned Standard had copied their design of the GAZ-Pobeda, which came out about a year before the first Vanguard.

The firm had named the model after HMS Vanguard, hoping that the British and

Commonwealth public, so keen on the Navy, would buy it by association.

It gave us a chance to get out and see much more of Berlin, and I got to know all three Western Zones of the city well.

I also had time to roam the camp, and found that there were damned near as many rabbits as there had been at Digby.

I found a gun shop in town, close by the ruined Kaiser Wilhelm Gedächtniskirche and bought an air rifle, a .177 Weihrauch, the most powerful air rifle in the world at that time, and deadly accurate. It was an amusing name for a gun, since Weihrauch, the German name for incense, literally means 'Holy Smoke'.

Early mornings and late evenings I and Chris, who used the Anschutz .22 rimfire obtained for us by Herr Dorsch, the camp Dolmetscher, began to cane those rabbits, and we were soon eating them and supplying them to all and sundry, including the officers' mess.

Not content with that, I found places in Berlin where there were a lot of ducks, though I had to be careful that there were no witnesses when I poached them.

Even bigger pleasures were the Havel, a huge lake, close by, and the British Berlin Yacht Club, of which we became members and keen sailors, spending many memorable hours out on that broad expanse of water under the flaming Berlin sun.

It could be tricky sailing at times, because the wind always seemed to swirl around that stretch of water, probably because of the surrounding hills.

During my teenage years I had done some crewing for a friend, who had a large keel boat on the Broads, and was somewhat familiar with the workings of a yacht, but had never sailed a small dinghy on my own.

We practised in Olympic dinghies, one man jobs, and passed our tests in them, then went on to Pirates, which would take a crew of two. There were larger boats also, including the Star Class, which were rather large. The one named '*Wansee*' was rightly famous, for it had won the 1936 Olympics in its class for Germany. It and all the others had been appropriated as part of the reparations at the end of the war. One of the best sailors in the Club was a 15-year old lad, Martin Wolf, whose father was a German 'works and bricks' guy living on the camp with his family. Martin was one of the best sailors in the club and spoke better English than most of us. Chris sailed with him and also with Jimmy Punt, one of the Russian linguists. Another excellent sailor, a civilian draughtsman who worked on camp, was often in the clubhouse, but was always inebriated. The story goes that one day, desperately needing a pee, he blithely took the top off the pot belly stove in the club house and urinated in it. The fire was well alight, and his efforts produced huge clouds of steam, which carried a certain instantly recognisable aroma. There were women in the clubhouse at the time too. Another memorable character!

Later I was to sail a great deal, qualifying as a sea-going skipper, and racing an International 505 that I owned for several seasons off the coast of East Anglia, at Lowestoft; a really hairy boat, with the largest sail area to size of boat of any in the world. One needed a crew weighing at least 14 stones, even in a force three, and it was wet-bottom sailing at its very best.

The three of us, working together in the section, and spending quite a deal of time together outside of it, became known to many of the GSO personnel as '*Die unzutrennliche Drillinge*' – the 'inseparable triplets', despite diverging interests on the part of the Third Man. That pseudonym would later be seen to have been ironic in the extreme.

By that time we had the job down to a fine art, logging far more intercepts than we had at the beginning, and we were becoming dab hands at locating the outstations and getting them DFed while they were still on the air as well. From the congratulatory signals we received from GCHQ, we knew that they appreciated our efforts.

At a later stage, speaking to one who should know, I was told that those DFs had allowed several agents to be located and arrested.

Whether he was telling me that merely to make me feel good, I have no way of knowing, but it was perfectly feasible.

The HVA, the East German foreign intelligence service, which was under the control of the Ministerium für Staatssicherheit – the STASI – was feared for its excellent capabilities in the field of human intelligence – HUMINT – and had a huge number of agents operating not only in West Germany, but in all the western nations.

I guess one spy here or there made very little difference to their grand, overall plan.

Jacquie's pregnancy had progressed well, and in due course she went into BMH, the British Military Hospital in Berlin, to have our baby.

Chris' wife, Helen, was due at the same time, but since hers was a 'blue' baby, she was flown to Rinteln, in the British Zone, where they had a specialist unit.

Chris and I, used to visiting *Zum Dorfkrug* a couple of times a week, visited it more often for a few days and stayed longer. On a couple of occasions, we were the only customers, and I wondered how Liese, the Wirtin, managed to keep her head above water. When I asked her, she smiled and said she got by.

She was well educated and had helped me a lot with my German, correcting me when I went wrong, and by that time my vocabulary almost matched that of my native language. What I didn't realise then was how bad my grammar was, since I had never tried to learn it. The gender of most nouns I knew from repeated use, but of the cases I had not a clue, though I did usually get them right, without knowing why.

After a couple of days, Chris obtained a flight, in order to be with Helen when the baby was born, and went to Scharfoldendorf for the time he was in the Zone.

There, he met a recently promoted sergeant in the Code and Cypher Section who'd been on the same Boy Entrant course that he had and had the same seniority as a corporal. He told Chris on the QT that the signal that brought his own promotion had also brought ours, but that Flt Lt Bill Cheek, our CO, had stopped them and declared that he, *'didn't want any more bloody sergeants on the unit. He had enough already.'*

When Chris came back and imparted that little snippet of information, we were as livid as he was, but what to do about it? We couldn't put in for redress of grievance, saying we knew our promotion was through and had been withheld, because the signals lad would have got into so much hot water.

Instead, each of us put in a general application for a posting, all worded identically, stating that we believed that our present job was holding up our promotion.

Surprise, surprise! Suddenly, our promotion to substantive sergeants was promulgated!

Bill Cheek obviously knew the hoo-ha that would arise if GCHQ found out that we were unhappy.

For all that, he was a grand CO, and we all liked him. He no doubt had his crosses to bear.

Always on the lookout for a way to make an extra pound, I found out that the Americans held an auction once a month, selling off their military vehicles. There was not much interest and they were sold for a song.

Of course, the lorries and vans were of no interest to me, but I began to buy the odd car and sell it on for a profit on camp. It was a sideline that I would continue with for almost the whole of my service and for many years afterwards, learning how to rebuild engines, gearboxes and back axles, trace electrical, mechanical and fuel faults, repair bodywork to professional standard and respray vehicles.

The Corporals' Club had a Christmas raffle each year, and a great many tickets were bought, but the raffle was a poor one.

I hadn't taken much notice the first year, but there were great rumblings among the members that the prizes were a poor offering, considering the amount of money that must have gone in. There was much talk of fiddles.

Other functions where money was concerned produced similar results, and there was a lot of talk about removing the committee and replacing the members. They were deeply entrenched, and had been in office for three years.

The old adage was true in their case: familiarity had bred contempt.

To cut a long story short, we voted them out and the three of us took on the job.

Promotion of the Christmas Draw went so well that there was well over a thousand pounds to spend on prizes.

We were approached by the previous committee members with open pleas not to make too much of a success of it, because it would make them look bad. If we had needed convincing, that clearly told us that they had been fiddling the books. We took no notice.

With the amount of money we had available and standard price prizes it would have taken all night to draw the tickets, so we decided to have a new car as the first prize, and about fifty other good ones, none of less than ten pounds in value and most around thirty.

It was a great success, with a whole lot of questions being asked about previous draws, but, of course, someone had to complain.

Too much money had been spent on the top prize, and many more could have been bought instead, it was claimed.

The following year, with over three thousand pounds available, we did as suggested, and the general moan was that there was not a car as first prize.

People!

In our third year at Gatow, Chris got talking to a mechanic in the MT section.

He regularly went over into East Berlin shopping in his private car.

Those service personnel not employed on secret duties and their families were allowed to visit East Berlin, and bus tours were regularly arranged. Everyone was supposed to cross via Checkpoint Charlie, situated in Friedrichstadt at the junction of Friedrichstrasse with Zimmerstrasse and Mauerstrasse (the latter turning out later to be an apt name for the place, since it meant 'Wall Street'), the only crossing designated for the Allied Forces to use.

We, of course, doing the job we did, were totally banned from crossing into the East.

Chris went across with his mechanic friend and made some purchases.

He got away with it, and we began thinking about the possibilities and the problems.

One of those problems was that the Security Services did regular checks on all personnel involved on secret work, and I had been sure I was being followed on a number of occasions, both in my car and on foot. After thinking I was becoming paranoid and imagining things, another sergeant told me in conversation and without prompting that he was certain he'd been followed, and after that I watched assiduously every time I was out in the car. They were clever and did the old 'switcheroo' routine, but I had noticed the same cars hanging back two or three cars behind me on several occasions and recognised them more by the fact of how inconspicuous they were in shape and colour than by anything that stood out. It was an accepted part of a 'Y'-service operator's life, though never acknowledged openly by anyone. I believe now that every serviceman employed on the intercept unit at Gatow was followed for a period at some point during his tour. In hindsight, the Security Services were right to be paranoid. I am convinced that I was also followed for a time in England on two postings.

Both Chris and I have a wild streak, and the thought of doing something so audacious was highly attractive.

Chris had recently learnt to drive, and had bought an Opel Rekord saloon.

My Vanguard would stand out like a cockle on a rock if we used that, but the Opel, being a standard German model, would not.

One great attraction was that it was possible, though illegal, to obtain an exchange rate of anything up to six East marks for one Deutschmark.

The standard exchange rate was one for one.

We were paid in BAFVs, British Army Service Vouchers, and used them for all NAAFI purchases, but were able to exchange them for marks, at the rate of twelve marks to the pound.

One morning, feeling like naughty little boys, we visited a money-changer on Kantstrasse, in Charlottenburg, coming away with wads of strange looking notes.

Looking back, we must have been utterly mad, because if we had been brought up on a charge of crossing just once we could have received severe reprimands and possibly been thrown out of our jobs and the 'Y' Service.

We just thought it a bit of a lark.

At first, that is just what it was, and what we bought was for our own use, but as we found more shops willing to sell to us (all of them were strictly forbidden by the stringent East German laws to do so and could have got into tremendous trouble if found out, the only one permitted to trade with

Forces visitors being the official government shop), we began to buy things to sell on.

Everyone on the base wanted a 35mm camera, but they were expensive things.

We found a shop in the Behrenstrasse that would serve us, though both the woman and the man who ran it were as nervous as kittens every time we were in the shop, one always remaining by the window, head turning constantly, anxiously scanning left and right, looking for one of those ubiquitous, green and white Volkspolizei cars to turn the corner into the street. I've often wondered what they would have done if one had been seen. I guess we would have been bundled out of the premises, accompanied by cries of 'We cannot serve you! It is strengsten verboten!'

They had a line in Werra cameras, a strange looking but highly efficient 35mm, made by the famous firm of Carl Zeiss, Jena, whose unusual lens cover, when turned round and screwed back on, became the lens hood.

It also had an unusual and unique method of advancing the film and cocking the shutter. This was achieved by turning the knurled ring at the base of the lens ninety degrees clockwise.

I can't remember now what we paid for one, but at the exchange rate of six to one they were cheap as chips.

We had decided that when we sold anything we would work on just one hundred per cent mark-up, instead of the five hundred per cent we could have asked for, so that everyone was happy and got a real bargain.

In the Schützenstrasse we visited a porcelain and glass emporium, which Chris had been to with his mechanic friend, and bought loads of beautifully crafted Meissen, Dresden and Karl Ens porcelain birds, puttees, animals and small statues, as well as Murano-type blown glass figures, animal bands, gorgeous vases and drinking glasses, a set of the latter of which I used just yesterday when visitors came. They are quite large, capable of holding almost half a pint when full, beautifully engraved, with heavy knops on the baluster stems, giving them the appearance of glasses made during the seventeenth and early eighteenth centuries, and they are always deeply admired.

The quality of the items was unequalled, and we had waiting lists of customers wanting anything we could lay our hands on, some of them senior ranks.

Our little set room now had a secondary purpose – as our shop, and when its doors were thrown open our large cupboard had the appearance of Aladdin's cave.

For months, we went over the border at least twice a week, and business boomed. Our boast was, 'You want it, we can get it for you.'

It was at that time that one of our customers gave our enterprise the nickname *'Murder, Rape and Arson Incorporated'*. It stuck.

The business was the worst kept secret and, of course, there had to be a reckoning.

Until that time I had never owned a decent camera, but with trading them I became interested in photography, a hobby that became almost a trade.

I took hundreds of photographs.

Colour printing was at that time an extremely difficult procedure, tackled only by professional firms, but in East Berlin we were able to buy the chemicals to do it, manufactured by the firm of Agfa, and I took up the challenge.

One of the officers, learning that I was keen on photography, told me that down in the cellar of SHQ was an old enlarger, which had been the one used by the Luftwaffe when they flew from Gatow and which no one wanted - one of really excellent quality, but huge and heavy. He asked for permission to give it to me, and with it I began producing black and white prints in enormous quantities, but colour printing was something else entirely – a real challenge.

For one thing, there were at that time, instead of the two-bath developer and fixer used for black and white, seven different baths one had to push the colour prints through, with a much tighter temperature range and length of time in each bath. Nowadays, the process is much simpler.

Worse, whereas with black and white one could use a red safe light to work by, one had to work entirely in the dark with the colour prints.

With the length of time the print was in the baths, it meant that doing a test strip to ascertain what exposure to give the prints took almost an hour.

If the test strip was over or under exposed, the next exposure time had to be guessed at and another hour went by before one could be sure of success.

Only when a perfect test strip was obtained dare one go ahead and print the pictures on the reel.

Photography almost took over my life, and I was soon doing developing and printing for half the station.

Very often, I was in the cramped little dark room I had contrived under the eaves of the mess above our flat until three in the morning.

No wonder I looked washed out sometimes.

CHAPTER SIX

One day, coming out of Summit House with the shopping, I was approached by a scruffily dressed English guy who asked if I had a packet of fags he could buy off me.

He was in civvies, and I asked why he didn't go into the      NAAFI and buy himself some.

The story he told was that he had been demobbed from the British Army in Germany at his own request, and had been living in East Germany.

He had married a German girl there, and had worked as a labourer, but the Vopos had begun sniffing around and things had become dodgy for him, so he had fled to the West.

He said that he, his wife, and his baby were living on crumbs and handouts in hostel accommodation.

I gave him a couple of packets of cigarettes, and he asked if I could get him some coffee, for which he would pay me, so that he could trade it for other goods, particularly baby clothes.

Our own baby and Chris' were out of baby clothes by then, but we still had them, and I could see no reason for not giving them to him. I hated to see someone so down on their luck, though I was not naïve enough to believe every bit of his story and, in retrospect, I should have listened to my conscience: that wee, small voice that tells you you are about to be caught.

I told Chris about him, and between us we rustled up a bag of food and all the baby clothes and took them to him on our way East one day.

One night a week or so later when I'd been on late watch, I had crawled into bed about quarter to one, only to be disturbed shortly afterwards by the cries of my daughter, Sheron, (my story is that we were going to have a boy and name him Ron, but when it turned out to be a girl....)

I had settled her down and finally fell into a deep sleep when, at quarter to five, there was a hammering on the door, accompanied by loud shouts, as if all the hounds of Hell were baying to get in, and I staggered out of bed, still three parts asleep, pulled on a dressing gown, since I slept in the nude, and opened it, only for my arms to be grabbed immediately by two huge 'snowdrops'.

One of them growled, 'You're under arrest' but would not tell me what for.

Though I was unaware of it, the same thing had happened to Chris.

They did let me dress, standing beside me to make sure I didn't jump out of one of the first floor windows.

Jacquie, bedclothes pulled up to her chin, was petrified, not knowing what was going on, and probably wondering what I had been up to without telling her; quite aware of my predilection for doing things that were 'on the fringe or beyond'.

Once dressed, I was bundled down the stairs and out to a waiting Volkswagen.

At the rear of the guardroom were a number of cells on a long corridor, and I was put in the first one inside the door, while Chris was put in the one farthest away from mine.

I was interrogated by a Flight Sergeant SP for almost an hour about our visits to the East before he left the cell.

He had given nothing away.

I had avowed that if there was any charge to answer, I was fully responsible, and that Chris was in no way to blame.

Chris, for his part, said exactly the same thing, but insisted that I was the completely innocent party.

Breakfast time came and went without the slightest sign of something to eat or drink and another interrogation began.

Throughout the day it was like that, one hour of questioning and an hour of solitude, repeated ad nauseam.

No lunch came up either.

I was allowed to go to the toilet at one stage, accompanied by a sergeant snowdrop, who did not take his eyes off me.

I don't know if he thought I had a poison capsule I was going to take, but he looked mighty suspicious.

More interrogation and no tea.

At seven o'clock in the evening the Flight Sergeant came back in, sighed heavily and declared, 'Both you bastards have stuck to your stories like glue; you take all the blame and he takes all the blame; you're like a couple of bloody parrots.' He sighed again and went on in a softer tone, 'Look, we know every date and time you entered and left the East, which shops you bought from and what you bought. We know all of that part of it. Now, you know and I know that I could throw the book at you for your sorties into the East and your black market dealings, but I couldn't give a shit about any of that. We are only concerned about one thing.

You've admitted meeting this guy, Albert Slade, as he said his name is, and gave him baby clothes, coffee and fags.

His name is not Albert Slade. He's Graham Woollard and he is an East German spy. He was not discharged from the Army, but deserted and fled to the East. What we want to know is: did you ever once tell him what your job is or give him any information about what you do here? That is all I am interested in.

Well?'

I re-iterated my statement, which was perfectly true. Slade, or Woollard, or whatever his name was, had never made the slightest reference to work, and, of course, if he had, we would have immediately reported him. We were not stupid.

The Flight Sergeant sighed again, shaking his head.

'Go on,' he offered, jerking his head at the cell door. 'Piss off and get something to eat. You must be bloody starving. I am. Sorry about that, but it was your fault, you know. And,' he added, 'for Christ's sake don't go anywhere near the East again.'

Chris was coming out of his cell as I exited mine and we exchanged amazed looks.

We waited until we were outside before speaking.

For days, we expected to be charged over our trips to the other side and our racketeering, but nothing was ever said.

It was over a year later that we learnt who had caused us all that bother – our supposed good friend, the Third Man. Some inseparable triplets!

The saddest thing is that he did not shop us out of any sense of protecting the national interest; it was from pure jealousy.

If you are still alive and happen to read this, S, neither Chris nor I have ever forgiven you.

Our tour was over just two months later, and we realised we'd got away with it, thanks to that kind-hearted Flight Sergeant.

I was quite devastated to hear a report a few weeks after returning home that he had been caught in a compromising situation with one of the maids and was facing the end of his career.

He signed a revolver and ammo out of the armoury and shot himself in one of those same cells.

Poor bastard!

CHAPTER SEVEN

I was posted back to Digby and Chris to the training school at Wythall.

To travel home by car we had to drive through the East Zone; a harrowing experience.

First of all one had to be issued with 'Flag Orders' the ПУТЕВКА – a document in English, French and Russian, the details of which had to agree in the most minute detail with one's ID card, vehicle number plates and so on. As little as a comma in place of a full stop would have one refused passage.

One drove to Checkpoint Alpha at the beginning of the East Zone stretch of autobahn, which apparently had never been repaired since the Hitlerzeit, the concrete surface cracked and potholed along its entire length.

We had to drive in convoy, and at least one of the vehicles had to be manned by personnel who were not security cleared, and we were not allowed to stop at all during the journey to the Western Zone at the Helmstedt crossing point – Checkpoint Bravo.

The speed limit for the trip was 50 miles per hour, which under no circumstances was to be exceeded. Drivers had between two and a half and four hours to make the journey, and if a vehicle had not arrived after four hours, military police would be dispatched from Checkpoint Bravo at Helmstedt to look for it.

We were briefed before leaving, being told that we were to have no dealings under any circumstances with East German police, since they were not officially recognised. If one did have dealings with the other side, they had to be uniformed Soviet military. The travel document, which had a Russian translation included, must not be altered, folded or damaged.

We were also given a printed notice to read, which told us that we must report any attempt to speak with us during the journey.

It stated: *"Should you be spoken to by a Soviet or East German national in English or a language you understand during your journey on the corridor, you should do the following:*

*Remember as much detail about any conversation that you can, as well as the physical description, dress and rank of the official.*

*Remain non-committal throughout and do not agree to anything.*

*Do not become overly nervous or aggressive.*

*Once it is realised that you are not responding, you will be left alone.*

*Remember: Do not attract attention to yourself by speaking in Russian to the Soviet personnel at the checkpoint."*

Though incidents were rare, they did occur, but luckily not with us.

Our cars were inspected and checked for defects and for full fuel tanks, spare tyre (fully inflated), and the necessary equipment for changing a tyre and carrying out any other necessary emergency repair. The milometer reading of the vehicle was noted, as would be the time of departure from Checkpoint Alpha.

Next there followed a briefing, which began with the instruction that on leaving the western checkpoint we were to drive one hundred and fifty metres and come to a stop by the East German customs police barrier, where a Russian soldier would meet us, direct us through the barrier and escort us to the Soviet checkpoint fifty metres further on.

We were then to park our cars on the designated centre strip, where the Russian soldier would inspect our documents and send us into the small wooden building on the side of the road.

Inside it, we were told, it would be almost dark and we would be under the severe gaze of both Marx and Lenin in their even darker frames. At one end there would be a small opaque window, on which we were to knock gently.

The window would open, and at that point we had to make sure that the sleeve over the hand that came out for the documents was wearing a Russian uniform and not an East German one or civilian clothes.

How in hell we were supposed to be sure of that we didn't know, but those were the instructions.

It happened exactly the way it had been described.

The hand came out and almost snatched the documents from mine, giving absolutely no time at all to check what clothing the arm was wearing.

Then the window slammed shut again and I was left in limbo.

We had been warned that they would make us wait at least ten minutes, and they certainly did.

Half an hour went by in that sticky atmosphere, and I felt like a criminal, which is what was intended, of course.

At last, the hand came out again, holding the Flag document and another barrier pass, and again I had no idea what uniform was worn.

At last I could step out into the fresh air and present the documents to the same Russian soldier, who indicated that I should get back into the car.

He then preceded me on foot for about a hundred yards, walking slowly, while I rode the clutch to keep to such a slow speed.

Then, he stood aside and waved me on towards the next barrier across the road, manned this time by an East German border guard.

To him I gave, as instructed, just the barrier pass obtained from the Russians.

He lifted the barrier and we were through.

The escorting vehicle sat on the side of the road a few metres farther on, waiting for my and Chris' cars to be cleared, smoke coming from its exhaust.

The driver looked in his rear view mirror and waved.

I pulled up behind him and kept my own engine running.

After another wait of over twenty minutes, the barrier was lifted for Chris, and as he came through the escort vehicle moved off.

The two of us followed.

Homeward bound!

We did a pit stop at the Windmill on the Autobahn near Beckum.

Run by the YMCA, it was the only British Rastätte on a German Autobahn, visited by just about every serviceman and woman who had ever passed there from the year that it opened as a British establishment in 1946 until the day it closed in 1971.

Probably less than one in twenty of the service personnel who used it knew anything of its history.

It already been in use as a mill for almost a century when the miller Johann Heinrich Brockhinke bought it in 1850.

When the Autobahn was being built, the intention had been to demolish it, but instead the Autobahn construction company bought it and opened it in March 1939 as a Rastätte, which they named the 'Alte Mühle.

After that stop we stayed overnight at a comfortable hotel near the Dutch border before pressing on to the Hook of Holland, where I was to catch the ferry.

Chris, bless his heart, followed me all the way to the port, going miles out of his way to do so, before driving down to Calais for his own crossing, since the Vanguard was giving me some radiator problems. Luckily, it had not boiled while we waited at the check point.

CHAPTER EIGHT

We made it home in good style and enjoyed a fortnight's disembarkation leave, during which time I traded in the old Vanguard, pleased to see the back of it, despite its valiant service, for a Ford Cortina, which we called 'the Wasp', since it was yellow with a black bonnet, before I drove up to Digby, finding it exactly as I had left it three years before, apart from the different RAF faces in the set room.

The Soviet Air Force nets the boys in the set room were tasked with covering had not changed, and I remembered them well enough to slide easily back into my role as a deputy controller.

The RAF lads at Digby were a great team; and I remember them with affection. Some I would come across and work with on other postings over the years. They included WOs Reg Dudley, Ken Burrell, Joe Peachey and Jock, 'Ach, ma grannie's arse!' Dempster, the NCOs Bernie Tripp, Chas Crowley, who always liked demonstrating his sleight of hand and simple but entertaining magic tricks, Chris Stone, 'Ginger' Guerin, Bill Cody and Jim McTavish.

There were so many others, but my memory is, sadly, dim. I can still see their faces, but can't remember their names.

The civilians, particularly those who were into racing, were still mainly the same ones I had known on my previous posting to Digby, and greeted me cordially, asking if I had any tips.

I told them I would be working on the system again, now that I was back in the UK, but I found it far from easy.

Whereas before, two year olds were not raced until the first of March, I found that during the intervening time they had begun to race all year and over the longer distances too.

The system still worked to some extent, but it was harder work and less rewarding.

The gun club had, since my previous tenure, fallen into disuse, and I applied for and was granted permission to run it again.

I bought another polecat ferret, a delightful, very affectionate little creature, which I named Elsie and kept in one of the unused Nissan huts on the airfield, and started once more on the clearance of the rabbits, of which there were now hundreds.

They had obviously been making up for lost time in my absence, the randy little devils.

I also visited the Crop Dryers' base, hoping to get some more pigeon shooting, but they had stopped growing peas in Lincolnshire, and the gamekeeper was a new one, who viewed me with suspicion and told me they had no need of my services.

His belligerent attitude determined me to poach a few of their pheasants, which came over the fence to roost in the trees bordering the aerial farm, and I used the air rifle to do so. The trees were well inside our perimeter fence, so the birds legally belonged to the RAF the moment they came over onto our property.

There was also a small wood behind the post office, which did not seem to belong to anyone, although I guess it must have done, and there were often more pheasants than leaves on those the trees at dusk. Another good source, and, I foolishly imagined, safe from gamekeeper trouble.

One night, however, as I picked my way soundlessly into the wood, or so I fondly thought, though anyone who has ever tried to do that will know that one cannot avoid treading on and breaking a dead twig or two, I heard another body crashing out of the other side.

From the noises made I knew it was not a deer or another wild animal, but a human being, and I guessed it had to be another poacher, scared of being caught.

The episode did not put me off, and the post office wood supplied me with several dozen pheasants that year and the next, but I made it severely off-limits after the local police constable, who was renowned for being hard on poachers, was beaten almost to death in that wood by someone one night when he had tried to arrest him for poaching.

The attacker was never caught, and I wondered if it was the same man I had disturbed the year before.

Poor bloody bobby, and all for a couple of pheasants.

Those birds had a lot to answer for, since not only had they caused the demise of a police constable, who would, for the rest of his career, avoid poachers like the plague, but three times in the space of a year I had the front headlight smashed on the Cortina from birds flying into it.

With the cost of those headlights, they were damned expensive dinners!

Quarters being in short supply, I took on a private rental in the village of Ruskington, just three miles from Digby, mainly because of the wonderful fishing nearby.

The river Bain, a fast-flowing, shallow stream, held a huge head of chub, most of them over six pounds, and I soon found that I could have a terrific day's sport by long-trotting a one-inch diameter ball of mixed bread and cheese paste on a size six hook, with no float or weight.

They fought like demons, and I spent part of every evening there and often half a day on my days off.

There was another benefit: under the bridge some huge eels lived in the rocks, and particularly after a thunderstorm would take a worm.

Since they were only partly emerged from their hidey-holes and had half their bodies wrapped around rocks it was hard to yank them out, but I landed several in excess of three pounds; wonderful food, either fried or smoked.

Revesby Reservoir was also just up the road, renowned for its big fish, and there I caught my largest perch ever - a four-pounds twelve-ounce monster only a pound under the record and shortly afterwards my largest pike up to that time, one of twenty-seven and three quarter pounds, personal bests I never managed to beat until I landed a thirty-six pound pike on my fly rod a couple of years ago, after it grabbed the two-pound trout I was playing.

The reservoir had, all around it, huge willow trees growing in the water three feet out from the bank. They had been cut down to ground level to allow fishing to take place, but one had to fish out between the stumps, whose tangled roots almost filled the water around them, making the landing of a large fish extremely difficult.

It was a bitterly cold day, with low scudding clouds racing across the sky on the wings of an almost gale force easterly wind, which I was fishing directly into, and every few minutes a splatter of heavy raindrops hit my face like ice balls – a pike angler's ideal conditions!

I was fishing with live bait, the bait of choice of most pike anglers in those days; totally banned now, of course, and cast the line out thirty yards. Almost immediately, the float started bobbing wildly, indicating the presence of a pike near the live bait, causing it alarm.

Suddenly, the float went under fast and stayed under for around twenty seconds as the pike made its first run. Then, as always, the float bobbed back to the surface – the point where the pike reverses its hold on its quarry and swallows it head first.

I waited in anticipation, knowing that at any moment the float would disappear again as the pike moved off, unless, as sometimes happened, it had dropped the bait and swum off. I could hear my heart pumping as the adrenalin rush worked its magic.

Long moments passed, the only movement of the float caused by the waves, and I began to think the pike had gone.

Then, plop! The float disappeared, and I struck.

It was like hitting a solid brick wall, and I knew I had on a seriously large fish.

The battle lasted over three quarters of an hour, and each time I had the monster close to the bank it made another rush into the lake, looking for safety.

By this time every angler fishing the lake that day had reeled in their lines and come to watch.

I had several offers to gaff the fish, but declined them all. If anyone was going to gaff that pike, it was going to be me. Many anglers, though they would never admit it, are exceedingly jealous people when it comes to their sport, and I had no doubt there were those in the crowd behind me who would just love to 'misjudge' the stab with the gaff and knock the fish off. Gaffs are also banned nowadays, but were used by almost everyone in those days.

Doing it myself while playing the fish was not going to be a picnic, and while the pike did run after run I worked out my strategy.

Trying to bring such a monster to the bank through those willow roots would certainly mean losing the fish. I had to somehow get at least one foot on a root, so that I could gaff it in open water.

That was easier said than done.

I asked the guy standing nearest me to hold my left hand while I dangerously threw out my right foot, hoping it would not slip off the root when it landed, with disastrously wet results. There was also the possibility that I would drop the rod.

I managed the difficult manoeuvre and continued playing the pike, my legs wide apart.

The gusting wind almost knocked me off my perch half a dozen times during the next five minutes, but at last I had the fish beaten, and it came sliding in on its side.

The stroke with the gaff had to be dead accurate, or the fish would be in the roots and that would be that.

My heart beating fast, I jabbed the gaff down, and it was a perfect contact. I expelled the breath I'd been holding.

With the pike's head held out of the water, I had the guy on the bank pull me back to dry land.

A couple of dozen cameras flashed and kept flashing while I unhooked the pike and lifted it up in front of me with difficulty.

I had one of the men use my camera to take pictures and then slid the fish back into the water, to live to fight again.

What a day!

After six months on the waiting list I was allocated a quarter and moved into one in Cuckoo Lane – a dingy mid terrace, from which each morning and evening I was able to witness a highly amusing feat: our chief service policeman, 'Lofty' Copp, (I kid you not, that was his name) six feet four in height, wind himself somehow – I never worked out quite how – into his miniscule Morris Mini.

One leg went in, then one cheek of his bum, followed by most of his body, with his shoulders and head still sticking out of and above the top of the door. Then, unbelievably, his head was thrust down and the body disappeared into the car, the last leg was lifted, with the knee somewhere up near his ear, and the foot slid over the sill. When the door closed the entire front of the car seemed to be crammed with Lofty.

The same contortionist act was done in reverse, equally fascinating to watch, when he arrived home in the afternoons.

How he worked the pedals and drove the thing defied imagination, and why he had chosen such a vehicle to drive was beyond comprehension.

In September of my second year on that posting I was delighted to greet Chris Boyd again when he was posted to Digby, the school having moved there from Wythall.

He soon joined me in the poaching and ferreting and it felt like the old firm back together again, though without the dangers of the East Sector.

He loved the poaching as much as I did, and we expanded that activity. The hares we shot Chris would string up in the spare room at the back of his classroom, along with a few pheasants, to sell to the trainees when they went home at weekends.

Blood dripped all over the old furniture and the floor in that room, and how the hell he got away with it was a mystery.

It all nearly came to disaster one night when we went out as usual to shoot the pheasants after they had gone up to roost in the trees at the edge of the airfield.

As was our wont, Chris shone the light up the tree and I took aim at a pheasant, the rifle held steady on his shoulder for support.

Immediately, the night was turned almost to day when several vehicles that had been placed in strategic spots on Crop Dryers' land switched their headlights and spotlights on us.

Though the pheasants did not legally belong to them, we knew that if we were recognised and reported to the Commanding Officer we would certainly be stopped from shooting on the camp – something we wanted to avoid at all costs, so we dashed off at top speed and ran into the aerial farm, where we knew the location of every guy rope, and lay down on the wet grass between two bunkers.

Motors started up and lights swept over the whole airfield, back and forth, back and forth. We could see figures walking around near the trees where the pheasants were, but they didn't, in fact couldn't, come onto the airfield.

Those bastards kept it up for over an hour and a half, but eventually we heard them leave and clambered up, soaked through by the heavy dew.

Chris, who had and still has a wicked sense of humour, chuckled and suggested, 'Shall we go and poach a few pheasants now they've gone?'

Good sense prevailed, and from then on we gave those trees a miss from our predations, and concentrated on the post office wood and the few pheasants that used a couple of trees on the far side of the camp.

My request for an overseas posting finally came through. It was to RAF Butzweilerhof, Cologne, to which 5 Signals Wing had moved on the 30th April of the previous year.

Taking advantage of the chance to buy a new car without purchase tax, I traded the Cortina in for a new Ford Anglia 105E, the first Anglia to have an overhead valve engine.

It cost the massive sum of £412.

I chose to have a maroon one with a smoke-grey roof and felt like a king when I drove it out of the main dealer's premises four weeks later. With those colours it was one of the smartest little cars on the road.

Well before its delivery, and determined to avoid the rust that plagued all cars in those days, I hurried down to the ironmonger's and bought two gallons of thick, liquid Aquaseal, and the moment I got the Anglia home I had it up on the ramps and was underneath with a four-inch paintbrush, applying two thick coats.

Then I stripped out the lining from the boot, took all four door panels off and applied the Aquaseal liberally to the insides.

That car was as near rustproof as it could be.

I did that with every new car I purchased until the 90s, when the manufacturers had just about cured the inherent rust problems.

At 500 miles on the dot I changed the oil, and again at 1000, a process repeated every thousand miles until I sold the car with 125,000 miles on the clock. Those regular oil changes paid off.

An RAF motor mechanic bought the car and immediately stripped the engine to re-bore it, utterly amazed, he told me, to find that the cylinders had the same tolerances as a new engine. No re-bore was necessary.

CHAPTER NINE

Two days before I was due in Cologne I drove down to Dover and caught the ferry to Calais, making sure that I was early, worried that if I missed that boat and had to take the next one I would be late arriving at my new station.

I certainly needn't have worried: the E40 motorway, I found, ran all the way to Cologne from Calais, by-passing Brussels, Liege and Aachen, and I pulled up at the Butzweilerhof guardroom just before ten am.

The administration services on the station were first class, and by the end of that day I had completed the blue chit in the usual cavalier manner, visited 5 Wing, where I was welcomed by several old friends, put my name on the quarters list, hired private accommodation and arranged to bring my wife out a fortnight later. A pretty fair day's work.

With many well-known faces around me, the set room felt like home, and I soon fell into the routine, getting to know the details of the Russian and East German air force units that the unit intercepted, and their skeds.

A few days after arriving, I was approached by a beefy flight sergeant, Dougie Baxter, in the NAAFI one day and asked if I needed car insurance.

I didn't, since I had arranged it with my company, GCNU, before leaving England, but asked him why he wanted to know.

It transpired that he and his wife, Marge, were the sole agents for motor insurance on the camp, working through a broker in England,

and were making a decent extra income from it.

We got on like a house on fire, and they kind of adopted me, over the next couple of months showing me everything there was to know about the business, with the object of passing it on to me when their tour was up a few months later.

That time passed quickly, and I soon found myself the sole German agent for the highly respected firm of Hogg, Robinson and Capel-Cure.

Arranging policies for most of the clients I dealt with was dead easy, but the firm did not want newly qualified drivers on their books, for obvious reasons. I quite simply solved that problem by coming to a deal with a German insurance company.

Their rates were comparable, and I could satisfy everyone. Better yet, my commission from them was three times that which I was receiving from my English broker.

Dougie and Marge had not tested the waters with life assurance, but I asked Hogg Robinson if they were interested in selling that to the troops.

They leapt at the chance, and during the rest of my stay there I managed to sell £83,000 worth – a serious amount of money at that time.

Though I was quite happy to work merely for a one per-cent finder's fee, I found out later that an agent should receive ten per cent of the premium over the life of a policy. It would have set me up nicely.

Nevertheless, the extra money allowed me to sell the Ford Anglia and buy a new

Peugeot 404, which I began to use for rallying, after the usual rust-proofing, running-in procedure, and oil changes.

My wife and daughter arrived by plane at Templehof, and we moved into the private accommodation I'd arranged in Spandau, in sight of the prison where Rudolf Hess was still incarcerated and where he would remain until he committed suicide in 1987, aged 93.

Shortly afterwards, I had the opportunity to see at first hand an example of what I had always believed to be true: that the German mentality, so deeply imbued in them by Hitler's urging, was totally inflexible, something I had given the title, the '*Alles muss richtig gestempelt werden syndrome*' – (*Everything must be correctly stamped*).

It was my personal belief that it was a major contribution to their losing the war. We, the English, when confronted with a problem, would go out of our way to solve it, with no regard for regulations or any other difficulties. They, when coming up against the same problem, first considered what the officially laid-down rules were that governed their attempts to solve it, and would not under any circumstances contravene them.

The opportunity came when I was driving to camp from the private hiring very early one morning, following a fairly new Mercedes W180 saloon on an almost deserted road.

The guy at the wheel of the vehicle in front seemed to be a very good driver and was sticking to all the rules of the road. While I was following him we progressed a kilometre or so in good order.

At one point on that route the road dipped to pass under a bridge, and I saw ahead of the Mercedes a dark grey Opel Rekord, which was parked facing us at the bottom of the dip.

The Mercedes driver, having obviously seen the Opel, switched on his left hand indicator and began to pull out to pass it.

From that moment, I could clearly read his mind:

*"There is an Opel Rekord parked under the bridge.*

*I must pull out to pass it.*

*I'll switch my indicator on to advise the car behind that I am pulling out.*

*Hello! Just wait one goddam minute here! That Rekord is facing me.*

*The rules of the road state categorically that vehicles must be parked facing in the line of travel.*

*Therefore, that Rekord is not there. It has to be a figment of my imagination."*

At that point, he switched off his indicator, pulled back to the side of the road and drove without hesitation or braking straight into the parked car, which had probably been stolen and parked with its handbrake off, because it careered backwards across the road into the path of two approaching cars, whose astonished drivers had to take frantic action to avoid crashing into it, one going into a triple spin on the damp cobbles, before finish up facing the direction he had arrived in, and the other managing to come to a stop on the far side of the road. The Rekord wound up sideways-on across the centre of the road, after drifting back down into the dip.

I stopped behind the Merc, jumped out of my car and went to see if the driver was all right.

He was sitting at the wheel, looking stunned and muttering to himself.

Again I could read his mind: "*How could that possibly have happened? I hit a car that wasn't there.* "

He was obviously okay, and I returned to my car, weaved around the mayhem, not wanting to get involved with the police, which would have made me late for my shift, and left behind three very disturbed German drivers.

I could just imagine the clerk at his insurance company when he made the claim. I would have loved to see the wording.

On the other hand, perhaps they were used to their clients smashing into things that didn't exist.

I had known many Germans by this time, some intimately, and found that almost all of them had this attitude to the authority of the official written word.

Another thing was their inability to appreciate a good joke. Anything with the word 'shit' in it would have them laughing fit to bust, regardless of how unfunny it was, but a joke which needed a bit of thought, however hilarious an English person would find it, would leave them straight faced and looking puzzled.

Nevertheless, I enjoyed their company, and was determined to master the language now that I was back in the land of the Bockwurst und Kartoffelsalat.

One of the leading lights at 5 Wing was Warrant Officer Terry O'Toole, with whom I became close friends. He and his wife Guytane, who hailed from the Seychelles, and whose name was shortened to Gay by all and sundry, were great people. I loved hot curry and made and ate it regularly, but just one forkful of what Gay assured me was one of her 'mildest' curries, the first time I was invited to their quarter for a meal, almost blew the top of my head off and had me grabbing the water jug from the centre of the table and chucking its contents down my unbelievably scorched throat, to the open amusement of the other diners.

Gay's favourite sandwich was a slice of bread spread an eighth of an inch or more thick with sambal oelek, which is basically a mixture containing more than ninety percent chilli, and not just any old chilli, but the *adyuma,* sometimes called *habanero* – the hottest chilli in the world.

And she thrived on it!

She once handed me a knife on whose tip there rested the tiniest amount possible, to try.

I merely touched it with my tongue - and couldn't taste anything for the rest of that day.

Terry was Chairman of the Butz Motor Club, which ran rallies in the countryside around Cologne, and he got me to enter one, having shown me the types of instructions for the various stages, using map references and 'tulip diagrams', which showed road junctions at various angles, one of which roads would have a small circle on the end to show that it was the road that one entered by, and another with an arrow on the tip, indicating which road one should leave the junction by. Some were upside down or sideways, to help with the confusion.

The Sunday arrived, and around fifteen cars turned up at the start in a downpour, most with a driver and a navigator. I had my wife and baby beside me, intending to do the navigating and driving myself.

It was a gentle enough event, taking in about seventy-five miles of the Siebengebirge – the 'Seven Hills' - south-east of Bonn, on one stage of the rally coming in sight of its high point, the Drachenfels - the 'Dragon's Rock' - and the ruined castle atop it.

At each checkpoint, manned by cagoule-coated stalwarts of the Club, we were handed the instructions for the next stage, which I read and then followed.

Lunch was at a restaurant in the woods, followed by four more stages in the afternoon.

I found it delightful, came a close second and was hooked!

So began a sport and hobby that would be my main one for the next fourteen years, involving over a hundred thousand rally miles and a tremendous amount of fun.

Soon, I was involved in the running of the Club, after Pete Cousins, the Competitions Secretary, was posted back to the UK.

I had several ideas for other types of stages, and became adept at making up rallies that varied from extremely easy, for the Sunday drivers, to the somewhat difficult, for those who wanted more of a challenge.

On one of the easy days we had half a dozen entrants from the Bonn Embassy Car Club, to whom we had sent invitations.

Several of us had attended one of their Sunday jaunts, and had left them standing. They wanted revenge.

Three arrived in almost brand new E-Type Jaguars, and the rest in imposing Mercedes and BMWs, rally bars covered in badges on the front of all of them. All of the drivers were too-too, upper-class, gung-ho young chaps, silk scarves tucked artistically into their Saville Row shirts and accompanied in the passenger seats by beautifully made-up young ladies.

Looking at them, I was glad I had designed the rally in the very simplest way, with sections that had only tulip diagrams and map references, and had laid out the whole thing on main, tarmacked roads, as they did.

In the instructions for the rally, I stated clearly that all roads would be paved, and that if any unpaved roads were come across the crew should realise they had gone wrong and retrace their route.

Foolishly, I had imagined that the instructions were fire-proof, but then, I was used to dealing with ordinary, sensible people.

I explained to the Bonn drivers how to interpret the tulips, which they did not use, and after they had all insisted petulantly that they understood perfectly, making me feel like a moron, I pointed out that on the second morning section they should take special note of the instructions for diagram number four, which began, in block capitals, *'THIS IS A SPOOF INSTRUCTION. IGNORE IT COMPLETELY AND GO ON TO NUMBER FIVE.'*

It was a common thing that we did, to catch out navigators who were not concentrating enough, but that instruction was not normally written in capitals, and our members were never warned about it. I had used capitals to make sure that our Embassy guests were not caught out by it.

I sent off the first car, watched the rest leave, and ten minutes after the last competitor had departed I set off to drive the route to make sure that no one had broken down and needed assistance.

When I came to the third checkpoint, about an hour into the rally, Sally Chambers, wife of WO Bill Chambers, told me, 'None of the Bonn people have come through, Tony.'

'Shit! Where the hell could they have got to?'

I drove back to the first checkpoint and found that they had all made it to there.

Knowing instinctively what had happened, I drove the second section, following the instruction for number four – the one that should have been ignored - and the subsequent ones.

Any rally navigator with any savvy would have realised something was badly wrong when they came to the sixth tulip, which showed a five-way junction, since that was merely a T-junction, with only one of the two roads anything like a decent size. The other, which had been tarmacked at some time in the distant past, had weeds growing through the surface – weeds that had recently been knocked down!

With dread in my heart I turned down that road.

It became narrower and rougher, with trees encroaching onto it, almost brushing the sides of the car.

I drove around a bend and found them all stopped, nose to tail, the Jags in front and the Mercedes and BMWs behind them.

The whole bunch of drivers and navigators were standing together, gesticulating wildly and having a shouting match.

My immediate instinct was to back all the way out and leave them to it, but I just couldn't.

I drove up behind the last car and got out, to be surrounded instantly by the crowd, angry as a swarm of bees whose nest has been destroyed, and whose every member looked as if they wanted to lynch me. They had found someone to vent their spleen on and blame.

I took it for a few seconds, wanting to stick my fingers in my ears, but there was only one valid solution.

In my loudest parade ground voice I screamed, 'Shaddap!'

The silence was deafening. They had never in their lives been addressed in that fashion and looked stunned at my audacity.

I glanced around and picked out the driver who appeared to be the eldest, though he was no more than thirty-five.

I pointed at him and said, 'It's Alan, isn't it?'

He nodded, without speaking.

'Do you remember when I came up to you at the start with the instructions for this section of the rally and pointed out to you the part in capital letters that told you to ignore the number four tulip diagram?'

Grudgingly, he murmured, 'I remember you mentioning something like that.'

'Get the instructions from your car.'

I deliberately left out the 'please'.

He did so, and I told him to look at that instruction.

'Now, is that not clear enough? Your navigator ignored it, as did all the rest of your members, to each one of whom I explained it in words of one syllable at the start.'

The woman who had been in his car looked horrified.

He gulped and admitted, 'Beverley did not do the navigating.'

I was puzzled, 'Then who did – you?'

He looked around at his colleagues. Several of them were nodding at him. They wanted him to tell me something.

He sighed, 'That isn't the way we work, Tony. On all our rallies we sort of follow the leader. We can't see any point in everybody doing the work.'

'And who navigates for the leader?'

A tall blonde on the left hand edge of the small crowd began hopping from foot to foot, as if she was trying not to pee her knickers.

He pointed towards her, 'Deborah. She has some experience and navigates for Brian.'

She certainly had the look of a woman with experience, but not of the kind Brian needed that day.

I remembered being introduced to him. He had struck me right away as a know-it-all. He had got his come-uppance with a vengeance.

I felt like telling them that they were supposed to be the intelligentsia, but had shown no sign of intelligence. They certainly deserved it, but I let them off lightly. They had suffered enough humiliation.

I did re-iterate that they were entirely at fault, and that every one of the other rally drivers had completed the course without trouble, which I was not sure of, but assumed, and that they should back out after me and I would lead them to the restaurant for lunch.

Then they gave me the bad news!

The two leading Jags had each hit the same bad pothole and smashed both their sumps.

I heaved a huge sigh; they looked down on us as plebs, and maybe we were compared to them, but they had not been among the recipients when common sensse was handed out.

Shaking my head in disbelief, I suggested, 'You'll have to leave them here; locked up, of course. You can have them collected by a rescue vehicle later. Come to lunch.'

Alan looked around at the shaking heads. No way were they going to subject themselves to ridicule from a crowd of people they thought inferior to them.

'I think we'll pass on lunch, Tony.'

That did not go down well with me – I would have to try to explain to the restaurant owner why twelve of the covers I had ordered would not be used, but there was nothing for it.

It took some sorting out, there being very little room to turn round, but eventually, with the drivers of the two out-of-commission E-Types and their now not so attractive, pouting partners added to the crews of the still drivable cars, I managed to get them out of their mess and on their way back to the Embassy compound.

They never entered one of our rallies again, and I guess those E-Type owners recognised that although the cars were ahead of the herd, with better than seven seconds nought to sixty, rack and pinion steering, independent suspension on all wheels and disc brakes, to say nothing of looking terrifically sexy, they were not made for anything except the best roads.

Fifteen years later, after the company had stopped production of the E-Type in 1975, a Swiss friend of mine was making good money buying second-hand ones in England and taking them to Switzerland to sell.

I found that the Cologne police also ran rallies and made contact with their competitions secretary, Helmut Eismann, with whom I was to spend many happy hours drinking and chatting in his favourite Kneipe.

Together, we ran many rallies, and from him I obtained a genuine IPA – International Police Association – badge for my radiator grill, which confounded my brother, by then a sergeant in the Norfolk Police Force, since they were only ever issued to police officials.

It enabled me to do a lot of parking in restricted areas without getting a ticket.

Helmut also rallied in the German major rallies, and I went along as his navigator for a couple, and was then accepted as an entrant in my own right. They were serious events, with difficult forest and mountain stages, high speed sections, and good prizes, and quite a number of international rallyists took part.

As I entered more and more difficult rallies, I needed a navigator, and found one in Ron Matthews.

A recent arrival at Butz, it was rumoured that he had won a car in a magazine competition.

I asked him if it was true and he pulled a face and said, 'Yes, but it was only a tatty old Ford Anglia.'

We should all be so lucky, I told him and wondered if he'd ever heard of gift horses.

He was keen to learn to navigate, and we teamed up.

It was not long before we were cleaning up every prize in sight and gained such a reputation that often other drivers would look pissed off, get back into their cars and leave when we arrived, knowing that they were wasting their time.

To avoid some of that, we let it be known that we would change places, and Ron would drive while I navigated.

We still always took first place, and for two years running won the 'Driver of the Year' and 'Navigator of the Year' awards.

Those cups, and over fifty other awards, now grace the wall of my garage, long since relegated from the house.

Ron and his wife accompanied Jacquie and I on our weekly trips to Heerlen, just across the border in Holland, where almost all the Butz personnel went to buy top quality meat and vegetables at a third of the local German and NAAFI price, alternating between his car and mine.

We also acquired a taste for the Indonesian-influenced Dutch food specialities, like Nasi Goreng, Bami Goreng, Lumpia Goreng and the many dishes of the Rijstafel. I still cook them from time to time and can buy the ingredients from Holland on the Internet.

One day on a shopping expedition, we were stopped by two uniformed Dutch policeman, who stepped out into the road in front of Ron's Anglia, their right hands in the air, palms towards us.

He wound the window down, and one of the cops, his face as expressionless as the rear end of a horse, informed him, 'You ver speeding.'

'Was I?' Ron asked innocently.

'You ver driving at vone hundred and five kilometres per hour. Ve haf nefer seen such speed in a fifty kilometre limit.'

Ron was indignant, 'No. I couldn't have.'

The second cop chipped in with, 'You ver caught by radar.'

My sense of humour has got me into a lot of trouble over the years, and that day it caused some for him. I laughed and came in with the old English saying, 'Fiendishly clever, the Chinese.'

That went down like the proverbial lead balloon, and I had visions of the two cops reaching for the automatic weapons they had holstered on their belts.

They straightened up and the second one insisted angrily, 'Ve are not Chinese! Ve are Dutch!'

I couldn't help it, the situation was so ridiculous; I chuckled out loud and said, 'That'll cost you another fifty guilders, Ron.'

They gave us a ticket, still glaring angrily, and let us go with a severe warning to drive slower.

Nothing happened for six weeks, and we thought the matter had been forgotten or overlooked, but then Ron got an official letter telling him, in English, that he had been fined eighty guilders for the offence. A second note attached to the first said that there was the extra sum of a hundred guilders to pay for the English translation.

I had made a point of learning some Dutch, finding it very easy, since it was halfway between German and English, so I wrote a note in Dutch, which Ron signed, saying that since he spoke Dutch the translation was totally unnecessary, and therefore was not about to pay for it, and he sent off just the eighty guilders for the fine.

He never heard anything back, so they must have accepted it.

Almost all of the Dutch people I spoke to in their own language were delighted that an Englishman would bother to learn it, but just one reacted in a different manner.

He was serving in a camera shop, which I had entered to buy an ever-ready case for my camera.

I greeted him politely, held out my camera and asked for the case in Dutch.

He looked down his nose at me and proclaimed haughtily, 'If you were to ask me in English, I might be able to understand you.'

I was bloody annoyed. He asked for it and he got it.

In broad, run-together Norfolk dialect I demanded, 'He-yew-gotta-evaready-cairse-fer-my-camra, bor?'

He shook his head as if he had been hit in the face with a spray of lead pellets and had to admit, 'I didn't understand. Could you repeat, please?'

I ran it past him again at the same speed, and almost...well, almost felt sorry for him, but not sorry enough to let him off the hook.

He shrugged and said with a scowl that he still did not understand.

I smiled sweetly and in perfect Dutch said, 'Perhaps I should ask for what I want in your language.'

With the look of someone who has just been forced to swallow a very sour lemon, he nodded, and I repeated my initial request.

With bad grace, he rummaged in a drawer and came up with the required article.

I paid, bowed to him graciously and said, '*Thank* you.'

I hope it helped to cure his rudeness.

The trips to Holland were not the only journeys we undertook outside Germany.

Three times a year I drove down to Austria, and later Spain, on holiday.

In Austria we always stayed at the first place we tried, a private house in a tiny village called Münster, near the town of Brixlegg, on the River Inn. Mine host was Alfons, and his wife was Gretl, a deeply religious, lovely peasant couple.

Later, I was to take the whole of my own and Jacquie's families, and some friends, by minibus to the village, and one morning when I awoke I heard my father-in-law's raised voice, repeating one word, 'Mist!'

He had been a prisoner of war of the Germans, but had not learnt much of the language. As many soldiers of his era believed, one only had to shout an English word loud enough, and a foreigner would understand.

An early riser, he had gone out onto the balcony and looked out at the early morning mist which covered the valley, as it did most mornings.

I slipped out of bed and looked out of the window.

Gretl had also gone out onto the balcony next to him, and he was trying to make conversation.

She looked very uncomfortable as he kept repeating the word louder and louder.

I thought I had better intervene, opened the window and told him, 'You keep saying 'shit', Billy. 'Mist' means 'shit' in German.

To Gretl I explained, 'Er wollte 'Nebel' sagen, Gretl. Das englische Wort 'mist' bedeutet 'Nebel' auf deutsch.'

She looked highly relieved.

Billy, for his part, could not understand why I was making such a fuss about it. Having worked on the land for most of his life, 'shit' was a perfectly normal part of his everyday vocabulary.

The area, near the lake called Achensee, which was a fold in the mountains, 1500 metres deep, and therefore always ice cold, was a wonderful area for walking, and I loved to climb up to the alms, where the animals were taken to graze in the summer.

One day, having climbed the four thousand feet to the alm with the girl who would several years later become my second wife – the daughter of Jacquie's best friend - we walked past one of the rough huts the herders used for the cows and came across a quite old, scraggy woman asleep on a blanket – totally naked.

Her body was the colour and texture of old leather, with no lighter patches. Nude sunbathing was something she did regularly.

I couldn't help it – I exclaimed, 'Bloody hell fire!'

The woman woke up, saw us and reached frantically for something to cover herself up with, but must have left her clothing somewhere else.

She threw herself over onto her stomach, her arms tight over her sagging breasts.

She also must have climbed that tiny path all the way up from the shores of Achensee, just in order to worship the sun god.

It was while climbing that path on that day that I had my first heart attack, though I didn't recognise it for what it was.

My chest felt as if it was being crushed, and we stopped for almost a half an hour until the pain went.

It was years later that I found out about it, after my second infarction and an ECG.

As the book says, when it comes to heart attacks and traffic accidents, *"As long as you can walk away from them...."*

There was good fishing for brook trout in the tiny streams that ran down the mountains, and in the lake for char, which, I found, tasted very similar to rainbow trout.

On every holiday we ever spent there, the weather was always wonderful, with hardly a day of rain, no matter what part of the year we were there, but it could certainly be different.

I talked my brother into holidaying there one year. He had never been to Austria before.

It was pouring when they arrived and it poured continually for the ten days they stayed. The River Inn burst its banks and they were confined to the north bank.

He has never been back, although he now lives in Germany, on the doorstep.

Going there one year saved our lives.

We had a great holiday, but when we returned home late one Saturday evening and opened the door of the quarter we were almost asphyxiated by the air inside, our throats immediately burning.

I made my wife take Sheron down the stairs, while I foolishly held my breath and dashed through the hall and into the living room, where I opened all the windows, before dashing out again.

We walked outside and waited twenty minutes before attempting to go in again.

The air was still acrid, but was relatively safe.

On the living room window sill we had a run of sansevieria – 'mother-in-law's tongue' - which were almost as tall as the window when we left the flat.

All that remained of them were shrivelled, soggy bits of disintegrating plant material, burnt brown.

The coolant in the fridge system had leaked from a fractured pipe.

The expert I called in told me that had we been in the flat and sleeping when it burst we would all have died.

The drive down the Autobahn could also be fraught in many ways, and we soon learnt not to go during late July or August, when most of the German workers took their annual holiday.

Then, it could be nose-to-tail in all three lanes the entire way, and stop-start, turning a pleasant four-hour run into a nightmare twelve-hour horror.

The first year, not knowing that fact, we were travelling down to Austria and came over a rise to find all three lanes stopped in front of us, only a hundred yards down the hill.

I was in the outside lane and braked sharply, coming to a halt close behind another car. Worried that the next car behind me would not react in time, I started pumping the brake, to flash the brake lights.

Another car came over the rise behind me and skidded to a stop almost on my rear bumper. I could see the shock on the driver's face in my rear view mirror.

The family in the Volkwagen 1500 saloon on our immediate left was not so lucky.

A Mercedes came over the rise and the driver did not react in time.

It ploughed into the VW, slamming it into the Peugeot in front of it, killing all five of the occupants; a man and his wife, and their three children.

I and many other drivers and passengers leapt out of our cars and tried to pull open the doors of the VW, but the bodywork was so badly crushed that we were unable to do so.

The inside of the vehicle was a scene of carnage. The rear of the car had been so crumpled that the top of the back seats were above the head rests of the front ones; the children crushed underneath them. There was no movement and there was blood everywhere. It was quite obvious that there would be nothing we could do for the occupants, even if we could have got them out.

The Autobahnpolizei arrived first, in less than three minutes, followed by three ambulances and the fire brigade.

The police have helicopters in the air all day in the holiday season, monitoring the Autobahn traffic, and respond very quickly to problems.

It was a blazing hot day, and sitting on the side of the road without anything to drink we were wilted.

Not only that, we were all suffering from shock, though we were unaware of it at the time.

The Autobahn slowly cleared in front of us, but was blocked for four hours, we heard later. Before we were allowed to leave the scene we had to give statements, which were written out long-hand by one of the police officers.

That incident was by no means funny, but a more comical one happened on another trip.

Merc and BMW drivers are renowned the world over as people who believe they own the road and are entitled to right of passage over everyone else.

The journey in question was another when all three lanes were full, although everyone in the outer lane was travelling at around seventy to eighty miles per hour. It was early in our journey and we were only a hundred miles or so south of Düsseldorf.

Way behind me I saw a big BMW flashing to pass another vehicle, and over the next half hour or so it slowly managed to pass one and then another until it was dangerously close behind me, right up my backside.

I could see a large, florid, self-satisfied looking German driver at the wheel.

He flashed and he flashed, and I ignored him. Then he began to blast away with his horn.

I continued to ignore him, but after about twenty minutes I decided to do something about it.

I waited until there was just enough space between cars in the middle lane for me to weave in, let the BMW past, and squeeze out again behind him before the car following him could close the gap.

Then, for the next two solid hours, I sat behind him flashing my lights every few seconds and blasting away with my horn.

To begin with he kept holding his fist up angrily, turning his head to shout obscenities and braking hard and suddenly, but I'd been waiting for that and had stayed far enough behind and ready to brake myself to make that ineffectual. By the middle of the second hour he was lifting a hand up and waving it, saying, 'Okay, you've made your point. Please stop', then it was both hands in supplication.

I gritted, 'Oh, no, buddy. You don't get off that lightly.'

I carried on with the torment.

Eventually, in desperation, he indicated to pull across the inner lanes and left the Autobahn at the Stuttgart exit.

I had the distinct impression that he was only going off in order to come straight back on.

If he did, I thought, he would not be flashing any other cars that day.

I just hoped he had learnt a permanent lesson, but doubted it.

The third time we went down south, I decided to go all the way to Spain in late September.

Before doing so, I spent a couple of months learning some Spanish, and was glad I had done so, because we did not come across one Spanish person who could speak a word of English. Again, how times have changed.

It was most interesting as an experience.

Just over the border, when I had been driving for almost twenty-three hours, with just a couple of hours sleep on the side of the Autobahn, we came to an hotel, which my wife wanted to stay at, but it looked large and expensive, so I pressed on.

Shortly afterwards, we came upon a parador – a long-distance lorry drivers' rest stop with accommodation.

I parked and we went in. I asked the woman behind the counter for a room for the night and for dinner.

She looked amazed.

'Oh, your Honour', she insisted, 'our establishment is not good enough for you. Our accommodation is just for the camioneros.'

I told her that it would be perfectly good enough for us.

She shrugged and said that the cost was the equivalent of five shillings and included the evening meal and breakfast.

I paid her and she gave me a room key.

Affixed to the back of the door was the government list of charges they were allowed to make, and I noted that she had charged me double, which caused a smile. The hotel, if we had stopped there, would have cost ten times as much.

I love my food, but the evening meal, five courses, was more than I could manage, and the breakfast was similar in size.

From then on we always stayed at paradors when in Spain.

Now, of course, they have gone up-market and are only for tourists.

We motored down to the Costa Dorada and found a beach resort about forty miles beyond Barcelona.

There, I found plenty of apartments for hire, and took one for the equivalent of thirty shillings (£1.50) for a week.

As usual, I'd taken my rods with me and did some fishing in a little harbour. Beside me, an old lady with a hand line and a bucket of water was trying to catch something to eat.

I had bait, whereas she was fishing with pieces of crust.

I asked her if she wanted the fish I caught, and her thanks as she held my hand, almost weeping, snatched at my heart strings.

She told me that her husband had died and that with no income whatsoever her only way of feeding her three children was to try to catch fish.

They were desperately poor. There was no such thing as welfare.

I worked hard to ensure that they ate well that evening.

We had two miles of beautiful sandy beach for the week without a single tourist. Ah, those were the days.

The bodegas, similarly, were only patronised by the locals, and in them one was given a glass when one entered and could sample whatever one wanted, with no limit.

My favourite liqueur has always been Cointreau, and the first time we visited a bodega I kept re-filling my glass with it and downing it quickly. I must have drunk at least half a pint before going on to the other liqueurs and Spanish brandy.

When my vision blurred I realised it was time to go and somehow managed to drive out of the gate, before pulling onto a grass verge and sleeping it off for three hours - absolutely stoned!

I was drunk for over a day and had not bought a thing.

Later, finding one that did a fabulous dark red wine that the owner called his 'negro', which cost ten pesetas a litre (the exchange rate was 123 to the pound at the time), I regularly visited to fill up the five-gallon plastic containers I took back home.

One time, the owner turned the tap on to fill one of them and disappeared out of the door, taking the gizmo he used for turning the tap on out with him in his pocket.

The container started to overflow, making me want to get down on my knees and start lapping up that wonderful wine that was going to waste.

I tried to stop the flow by sticking my finger into the pipe but just got my arm sprayed for my trouble. Luckily, I was wearing a short sleeved shirt.

I was frantic at the loss of such wonderful stuff and started to shout for him.

He sauntered in about half a minute later, completely unworried at the sight of six or seven litres of spoilt wine on the floor.

When I tried to tell him I was sorry I had not been able to stop the flow, he shrugged nonchalantly and said, 'Now, if it had been water I would be worried, but wine...'

When we visited that bodega in later years on trips from England, I had narrower plastic containers holding two gallons that would fit inside the door panels; a trick that I got away with for years.

They were such wonderfully boozy days that often, when stopped at border customs posts and asked the question, 'Anything to declare?' I felt like holding my arm out and slurring, 'Here, take a blood test.'

CHAPTER TEN

After a year at Butz I was allocated a quarter, and was pleased not to have to do the daily commute.

It brought my wife and I into closer contact with the other personnel, and we were able to attend more of the parties, which took place almost nightly, alternating between flats.

Previously, we had attended a few, but since it meant driving home the worse for drink we had kept them to a minimum.

Once we were installed in a quarter, it became a regular thing a couple of times a week.

A whole lot of drinking went on, and in those days, like most of my contemporaries, I was close to being an alcoholic.

At one of them, which I attended alone, since our daughter was running a temperature and Jacquie had stopped at home to keep an eye on her, I had reached an advanced state of inebriation, although aware of the attentions of the attractive red-head beside me, whose chat-up lines were becoming very close to the mark.

Suddenly, she pulled my head round and began snogging me, her tongue working overtime, and then put her hand on my groin and squeezed, murmuring that she urgently wanted to have intercourse with me, putting the invitation very much plainer than that and in the vernacular.

It seemed only seconds after that that a well-built, highly tattooed, tough looking guy was yanking me out of my seat and directing me roughly towards the door out onto the balcony.

I feared the worst.

He closed the door behind us and growled belligerently, 'That lipstick you're covered in looks like my wife's. Is it?'

I told him I thought so, expecting to be knocked flat at any second.

He sighed and nodded, 'She's a fucking slag. It's not your fault, mate.'

Even in my severely inebriated state, I was astonished when he looked me up and down and pronounced, 'You know, you're just the sort of man we like to have in the Masons. I'm in the local Lodge and it's great. If you like, I can put you up for it.'

I told him I'd think about it.

When I was sober the next day, I wondered how many of the Lodge members had, as the Good Book says, 'known' his wife and been put up for membership by him as a result.

It was certainly a unique form of recruitment.

Often, those parties went on till the early hours, and sometimes it was obvious that the host wanted to go to bed but was too well mannered to mention it.

One of our lads, Ted Graham, had the answer to that one.

When the party was in his quarter, and he thought the time had come for his guests to go home, he would disappear for a couple of minutes and come back in wearing just his pyjamas.

It worked every time. Suddenly, his flat would clear of guests.

Ted was quite a kidder, and he caught me out nicely on one occasion.

He had ordered a new Renault Dauphine from the factory in Paris, and had to go there to collect it.

He asked me and another colleague to go with him to share the driving, the other chap to sleep on the way and then to drive his old Dauphine back to Cologne, and me to help driving there and back.

It was just on five hundred kilometres and we set off at midnight, with the boot full of five-gallon jerry cans of cheap petrol, bought with BZ coupons, to save buying expensive French juice.

I stayed awake, offering every couple of hours to drive, each time told by Ted that he was wide awake.

In the end, he drove all the way, and I had no sleep at all.

We arrived at the outskirts of Paris at six-twenty, and made it to the factory just before seven.

Parked up, we walked along the Avenue Gabrielle back to the Place de la Concorde, to watch the traffic, which had been bad enough when we'd driven round it, but which had picked up to incredible proportions as it approached the main rush hour.

Along that avenue there must have been two hundred cars parked, and not one of them without a bent wing or other damage.

At Concorde, in the space of a few minutes we saw hundreds of near misses, as drivers took their lives in their hands to join the traffic circumnavigating the island, which helped to explain the damage to the vehicles we'd seen.

We wandered back in time for the opening of the showroom, and Ted was handed over his brand new Renault.

He looked over it in minute detail and then pronounced, 'I'm totally knackered, Tony. You can drive it back home.'

Like him, I had had no sleep at all.

I said, 'Gee, thanks, Ted. You're a real pal!'

I was wondering what chance I had of getting round the Place de la Concorde with an unscratched new vehicle.

Miraculously, it seemed, I did, and apart from being as tired as a swallow after its four-thousand mile journey to its nest in the UK, managed the journey okay, but it was not without further incident.

Driving *into* France, the French customs had not been in the least interested in us, but when we tried to cross the border back into Germany at the crossing near Valenciennes, they made us get out and were all over the new car like a rash.

Ted, who'd been asleep all the way from Paris, grumbled sleepily when I woke him to deal with them.

Finding the jerrycans of petrol in the boot they started to treat Ted as if he had just raided the Louvre.

I let him get on with it; it was his car, for goodness sake, and I got back in and was dozing off in the driver's seat while he argued with them at the top of his voice.

They spoke no English and he spoke no French.

He kept telling them that the petrol was bought in Germany, and that seemed to inflame them even more.

One of them kept shouting, 'Il faut que vous payez la taxe!'

In the end, I staggered out of the car and told them, in French, how we were allowed to purchase petrol at a reduced rate in Germany; that we had brought said petrol into France with us and were now taking it back into the country where it had been bought. I could have understood if they had demanded tax on it when we entered the country, but could see no sense whatsoever in them wanting us to pay tax on the way out.

It fell on deaf ears. The same officer, addressed in his own language, calmed down, but informed me again, 'Oui, monsieur, je comprends, mais néanmoins il faut payer la taxe.'

In desperation, I asked him, 'Mais porquoi?'

Before he could answer, Ted, who spoke virtually no French, piped up with just one word, 'Militaire'.

It was the magic word.

The douanier's face cleared.

'Vous êtes soldats?'

I was not going to split hairs while we were ahead.

'Oui!' I told him emphatically.

'Eh, bien alors, vous pouvez passez. Bonne chance.'

If nothing else, the interlude brought me back to full wakefulness, and I managed the rest of the drive with no trouble, handed the keys to Ted wordlessly when we reached home and wandered off to my bed.

A fortnight later another friend asked if I would do a repeat performance when he went to pick up his new Dauphine.

I politely declined. Once bitten...

Shortly after the trip to Paris my promotion to substantive Flight Sergeant came through.

More money – what on earth would I do with it all?

CHAPTER ELEVEN

I seized every chance I had to speak with German natives, and at the beginning of the last year of my tour at Butzweilerhof, believing that I was just about fluent in the language, visited the Education Centre one day and spoke to the Flight Lieutenant who ran it.

He asked what I wanted, and I said, 'I'd like to take the German GCE.'

He pulled a face, groaned slightly and muttered, 'Oh, not another one!'

Opening one of his desk drawers he pulled out an old exam paper and threw it across the desk to me.

'See what you can do with that. You can use the room next door.'

It was a one and a half hour translation paper, and I sat down and got to work.

Twenty-five minutes later I re-entered his room after knocking.

He grinned, 'Given up? I thought so.'

I wasn't having that!

'No, sir. I've finished it.'

He looked suitably amazed and I quite roughly shoved the paper back over his desk towards him, to show him how I felt about his comments.

He began to read and quickly scanned the entire thing, before sitting back, shaking his head.

He exclaimed, 'My God! You've got a terrific vocabulary, but your grammar...it's non-existent. I don't think I'd ever be able to straighten you out. You've learnt far too many mistakes, and they'll be ingrained and impossible to eradicate.'

I asked, 'Can I try?'

He shrugged, 'How hard are you willing to work?'

'As hard as you like.'

'All right. The exam is in five months. Let's give it a go.'

He was brilliant at his job, explaining very clearly the rules of grammar in German, after checking that I knew what the subject, direct object and indirect object of a sentence in English were.

He drew me charts of the definite and indefinite articles in the nominative, accusative, dative and genitive cases, and another showing which prepositions governed those cases.

I learned them off pat, repeating them over and over as he said he had done when he was learning the language: DER DIE DAS DIE, DEN DIE DAS DIE, DEM DER DEM DEN, DES DER DES DER; MIT VON BEI SEIT NACH AUS ZU GEGENÜBER, and the rest, until I had them off pat, which surprisingly took only a few days, and was saying them in my sleep.

With his help, I managed a Grade One, having found the examination extremely easy.

After congratulating me when he handed me the certificate, he asked, 'What are you going to do with it?'

It was my turn to shrug, 'Put it in the drawer with my School Cert, sir.'

'No, you are not.' He insisted, 'You are going to do 'A' Level.'

I began to protest, but he was having none of it, and he helped with the four books I had to study, giving me an insight into what the examiners would be looking for in the answers.

Six months later I was the proud owner of a certificate which showed that I had passed that examination at the top grade.

Again, he asked me the same question, and again I gave him the same answer.

This time he astounded and shocked me.

'No, you are not. You are going to do a Degree.'

I protested that I was nowhere near clever enough, but he persisted and wrote to London University, the only English university that did External degrees, for the entrance requirements.

When he received them, we made an application, stating my present educational achievements, and I received a letter back telling me that I needed another language at 'A' level and, horror of horrors, either Latin or Greek at 'O' level.

I baulked at that, but he was insistent, and I agreed to do it, since he promised to help me with the Latin and the French 'A' level.

Disaster struck the following Tuesday, when he was suddenly posted back to England, apparently under a cloud, though what he had done to incur the wrath of the powers-that-be I had no idea. I found him a great officer.

Left to my own devices, and with just four months until the GCE examinations, I began to study harder than ever before.

Those four months were probably the most painful of my life, but somehow, working entirely on my own, I managed an 'A' in French and a 'C' in Latin. I applied the same rules to French grammar as I had to the German, learning them by heart, and that was to have an amazing effect in the future.

In a life that has included many successes, that 'C' grade in Latin, after just four months work, is, I believe, my greatest single achievement. I still don't know how I did it, learning off by heart huge swathes of the *"Commentarii de Bello Gallico"* – Caesar's Gallic Wars: *'Oh, pig, with propitious left foot, who visiteth the bank of the river......'* and other totally useless drivel, but it paid off.

Thus began five years of hard study that gave me stomach ulcers and brought on other problems, not least of which was the Male Menopause, which I can assure those of you who are too young to have experienced it yet, or those who don't believe such a phenomenon exists, that it is REAL AND FRIGHTENING. I went off the rails big time, which would eventually lead to divorce, but there were benefits too.

When I began to study, I considered myself something of a dunce, educationally speaking, but was quite astounded by the changes that occurred.

I found that the human brain can, literally, expand its ability to learn, and the more one learnt, the more one was able to learn.

As my studies widened, my brain became like a dynamo that had been fed more power. During those five years I taught myself Russian and Spanish and passed the Civil Service examinations at Interpretership level in German and French, at Linguist level in Russian and Spanish and at Colloquial level in Dutch. I also taught myself to play the piano, wrote my first novel, and completed at least one difficult crossword every day.

There were no such things as correspondence courses for university degrees or Open University in those days, and all I had in preparation for the Degree course was the reading list and copies of old examination papers I had purchased.

I typed copious notes, which I came across in the garage only a few months ago - dozens of folders - and finally destroyed, remembering how useful a fast typing speed was to a student and author, and for that I had to thank my RAF Telegraphist training.

I was hitting over 100 words per minute by that time.

The book had to be typed on an ordinary typewriter, with two carbons, in order to send it to an agent, and one single mistake on a page meant that the entire page had to be re-typed. The machine I used was a German Adler, and at the time the Z and the Y were in the German positions on the keyboard, which took some getting used to. I have to grin now at the number of times I typed 'Butyweilerhof' on letters.

Nowadays, the plethora of new authors do not realise how good they have it, with automatic spell-check and instant erase.

I thought it world shaking when the electric typewriter came out, and when the later models had the ability to erase it seemed the best thing since Eve made Adam bite the apple.

Now, it is like falling off a log. Any mistake in a hundred-thousand word text can be located and changed in an instant with the

'Find' facility, and it is the work of less than half an hour to publish an ebook on Amazon or Smashwords.

What with work, study, insurance deals and rallying, my days were crammed.

Terry O'Toole was posted home, and I was voted in as Chairman of the Motor Club. Then the Club Secretary followed in Terry's footsteps and no one would take on the post, so Yours Truly took that on too. Shortly afterwards, the Treasurer suddenly decided he no longer wanted the job.

I found myself running the Club single-handed. It was a lot of work, and though I still put on a rally every month, when I left Butz the Club folded. No one was interested enough to keep it going. A great shame, as it gave many people a lot of pleasure.

Poor old Terry died around twenty years ago. Gay joined him last year.

CHAPTER TWELVE

My tour at Butz came to an end, and I was posted to North Luffenham, in Rutland, whose station crest was a bow and arrow, the latter being a bolt of lightning. The motto was 'Swift to Reply'.

I knew before moving there that from 1959 to '63 the station had been home to 144 Squadron and its complement of PGM-17 Thor intermediate range ballistic missiles, and that the Joint Services Language School had recently moved there.

I was intrigued at the posting and wondered what job I had been fingered for.

It transpired that I was to replace a recently departed warrant officer as Chief Examiner for Trade Group 11A, with two sergeant assistants.

It was a complete change of role, but one that I enjoyed.

I checked through the results of examinations for the previous three years and found that the pass rate was always in the high nineties, which immediately told me that the questions, which were hardly ever changed, had become too easy. Candidates were learning the answers off parrot fashion, without having to put any thought into the process.

There was a bank of almost a thousand existing questions, and we set about revising the wording of many of them and introducing new ones, with a higher difficulty grading, bouncing ideas off each other as we did so.

Soon, I had the candidates facing a sprinkling of entirely new questions, like *"How would you recognise a boustrophedonic* callsign pattern" and *"For what purpose is a Bellini-Tosi antenna used?"*

The next set of results came in much lower, at seventy-eight per cent, which was just about right.

A huge plus to the posting came when I'd been at North Luffenham for only three days.

I was turning the corner near SHQ and couldn't believe my eyes when I came face to face with my old pal, Gerry Jermy.

He looked as stunned as I was and told me he had been posted there only a month before.

I asked him if he'd been doing any shooting.

He said there were loads of pheasants, but no, he hadn't.

I had a general application in for permission to form a Gun Club less than an hour later, and approval was given after I had been questioned by the Adjutant as to its make-up and intentions. I would nominally be in charge, which meant that I would carry the can if any problems came up.

Pheasants were out of season at that time, but Gerry and I did plenty of reconnoitring in preparation.

I had to promulgate the Club, and three other lads asked to join, all of whom said they had shot before joining the RAF.

I took them out for a couple of hours that weekend, ostensibly to shoot a few rabbits, but actually to check them for gun safety; found that they were satisfactorily safety conscious and told them they were acceptable.

The first day of the season was a Saturday, and we had a field day. There were pheasants everywhere, many of them wild ones that had bred on the airfield, and they flew very well. From one small patch of stinging nettles no larger than the size of an average living room thirty-one pheasants emerged, leaving us with empty barrels after dropping nine of them.

It was a windy day, as most days were in Rutland, with no hill between us and the North Sea, and it was good sport.

One pheasant I shall always remember from that day. It came over from a neighbouring farm about eighty feet high, flying into the teeth of the wind, and seemed to be in a fixed position, right above our heads.

Each of us in turn had two shots at it – ten barrels, and it was untouched.

We looked at each other, astonished, looked back up at the pheasant and allowed it to sail happily away in perfect health. It fully deserved not to be shot at again.

It was the first time I had come across such a phenomenon, but it does happen. Those birds are called 'cast iron pheasants'.

Though they appear to be at a standstill, they are not.

With a moving bird, one allows for the forward movement. Shooting at one that appears static, but isn't, that forward allowance is not made, and the bird is missed.

That pheasant was the first to come over from the neighbouring farm, though I expected to see more, since it was obvious that an organised shoot was being held on that land - we had heard several prolonged bouts of shooting from some distance away while we walked the airfield.

I was not wrong.

About twenty minutes later, there came a multitude of shots much closer, as the shooters moved to a field bordering the airfield.

Every one of the pheasants they missed, and there were many, came over us, and we decimated them.

There were angry shouts from over the fence, and soon angry faces and shaking fists.

They were not happy at seeing their bred and released birds brought down by common servicemen.

Rutland may have changed now, but at that time it was a very class-conscious county, and its upper class ruled it with a rod of iron. The county shoots did not include any common folk!

It was tough luck. They should have made their drive in a different direction.

We enjoyed the spectacle, expecting that a complaint would be made to the CO.

It was, and he had me on the carpet, but was smiling broadly when he told me, after mentioning that he had received the complaint, to 'carry on the good work'. He also added that he enjoyed pheasant if I would like to drop a brace off at his quarter now and again.

I made sure that he was well satisfied.

By the time the season had started I had been allocated a quarter at No.4 Derwent Avenue in Edith Weston village, close by the camp, and drove back to Norfolk to pick up my wife and daughter, intending to do the round trip.

We left home just after four in the afternoon, and both my wife and daughter were dozing as I approached the town of Wisbech.

Seeing a thirty mph sign ahead I slowed down from the forty I had been doing, since a marked police car had pulled out of a side road behind me, and I was doing only twenty-seven as I passed into the thirty area.

The fuzz stayed behind me for the next half mile, while I religiously kept the speed down.

Suddenly, his blue light came on, and I braked to a halt.

A uniformed sergeant got out of the vehicle and wandered up to my door.

I wound the window down.

He began, 'You were doing well over the limit when you entered the thirty zone.'

I looked him straight in the eyes and told him, 'You know that is not true, Sergeant. I was doing twenty-seven miles per hour. I saw you behind me way before we got to the limit. I would have to have been mad to exceed it.'

He changed the subject, 'Where have you come from and where are you going?'

They seemed like strange questions to me, but I told him.

He bent to look into the car, 'Who is that?'

Jacquie had fallen asleep next to the baby in the back.

'My wife.' I told him.

'Could you wake her up?' He asked.

'Why?' I demanded, 'She has done nothing wrong.'

Did he think I'd kidnapped and drugged her, I wondered?

'Is that your daughter?' He changed the subject yet again.

'Yes.' I told him shortly.

Once again he digressed, 'Did you know you have a brake light that is not working?'

Without hesitation, I told him, 'That cannot be. I checked all the lights on a walk-round before leaving home. I am a rally driver and always do that before a journey.'

'Nevertheless, the light is out.' He said.

I shrugged, 'Well, all right. That's no problem. I carry spare bulbs and fuses for every light on the vehicle. I'll change it.'

I got out, opened the boot, where I kept the spares, took off the glass and changed the bulb, which then worked okay.

He appeared to be satisfied and offered, 'Well, that seems all right now. I have to give you a verbal warning, but you will hear nothing more about the matter.'

I drove away thinking what a strange experience it had been, and when Jacquie woke I related the story.

It was five weeks later, when I had almost completely forgotten about it, that I received a summons to appear before the magistrates in Wisbech.

The charge: *'Failing to ensure that a light was working on my vehicle'*.

There was a note attached, indicating that since it was a minor offence it would be in my interest to plead guilty.

I was absolutely livid.

I was in the AA and contacted them immediately, asking for their solicitor to appear with me on the appointed date.

They too suggested I plead guilty, but I was having none of that.

On the appointed day I met the solicitor, a weedy looking individual not much older than a schoolboy, who gave me no confidence at all. I told him the defence I wanted to use and he was unable to understand it. He also tried to insist that I plead guilty.

I told him, 'No way!'

We went into the court, where three doddery old individuals, two men and a woman, all apparently in their seventies or eighties, sat on the bench, causing me to groan under my breath.

My case came up and the charge was read.

The police sergeant stood up and told an entirely different story to what actually happened and what was said by him at the scene – every bit of it lies.

He had stopped me, he said, because the light was out, and he, (out of the goodness of his heart presumably), had replaced it himself with one from his own supply and sent me on my way after informing me that I would be charged with the offence.

The solicitor stood up and began to make an absolute hash of the defence.

I pulled him back down, stood up and asked for permission to speak for myself.

The three characters on the bench looked dumbfounded and conversed in low voices among themselves before the chief magistrate nodded permission.

'I am charged', I told them, 'with "failing to ensure that the light was not working". Had I been charged with "Failing to have the light working" I would have pleaded guilty, but I had done everything in my power to *ensure* that the light was working by checking all round the vehicle before leaving home and having a spare bulb and fuse for every light on the car. No one could possibly have done more to *ensure* that it was working. Also, the police sergeant was not the one who changed the bulb. *I* did it with a spare that *I* carried. Could you please ask the police sergeant to clarify that matter?'

The magistrate looked at the sergeant who stood again and said it was possible that he had got mixed up over that. He looked poo-faced.

That, I could see, had them puzzled, as had my explanation. The chief magistrate asked me if I could expand on my statement.

I stated that in the RAF there was a very great difference between not doing a thing and not *ensuring* that a thing was done. The first was an extremely serious offence and the second was minor. I could see that it had still not got through to them and asked, 'Could I be allowed to question the police sergeant, Your Honour?'

He nodded again, and to make sure that they understood clearly what had happened, although he had already tacitly admitted it, I asked, 'Did you or I change the bulb?'

He looked cornered, almost afraid, I thought, 'You did.'

'Was it your bulb or my bulb?'

'Your bulb.'

'What were your first words when you stopped me?'

He looked stunned, 'How do you mean?'

'Were your first words not, *"You were doing well over the limit when you entered the thirty zone"?*'

His face bright red, he looked down at the notes in his evidence book.

'I don't remember.'

'You don't want to remember!' I was getting nicely wound up, 'You will also, I am sure, not be able to remember that, as a parting gesture, you told me that you were giving me a verbal warning and that I would hear no more about the matter. I would not be charged with the offence.'

He was flustered, 'I'm afraid...'

I interrupted him, 'Of course you are, because every single piece of evidence you have given is a pack of lies.'

'Oh, now come on, sir...' He began, and the magistrate stopped him with a wave of his hand.

The old boy then conversed in whispers with his two colleagues for a few seconds before looking at me and pronouncing in a complete contradiction in terms, 'We have considered this case and feel that because your light was out we have to find you guilty, but are giving you an absolute discharge'.

They still hadn't understood the 'ensure'.

I glared at the police sergeant as we left the court.

Outside, as the solicitor and I were walking away, I heard pounding feet and turned to find the sergeant running fast towards us.

He stopped close by and grovelled, 'I must apologise to you, Mr Nash. I wish you had told me that your brother was in the Force.'

That made me good and mad.

'I didn't bloody tell you that because you would have thought I was trying to unduly influence you.'

'Oh, no, sir. Not at all. I do hope you'll forgive me.'

I'd had enough. I growled, 'Piss off! You're a disgrace to the bloody uniform.'

We turned and walked away, ignoring him.

He had good reason to be sorry he'd taken the case to court: he had been promoted for having such good numbers of proven cases; far more than his peers, but after I had told my brother about being stopped and what subsequently transpired, he had reported it to his father-in-law, who, unfortunately for the sergeant, just happened to be the senior officer at Wisbech and held the rank of Superintendent.

There had been quite a number of complaints by other drivers about incorrect evidence the sergeant had given in court, which had previously been ignored as a normal part of the public's annoyance with the police, but after learning of my experience, the Superintendent instigated a thorough undercover check on the good sergeant.

The officers involved contacted dozens of people who had fallen foul of him, finding masses of falsified evidence, and began to follow him, soon learning that on most days he was using his police vehicle to visit the wife of a fellow officer, with whom he was having sex while her husband was on duty elsewhere, blatantly parking the marked car outside her house.

As a result of those investigations, he was drummed out of the police force and lost his pension rights.

My brother told me that the ex-cop had got a job as a driving instructor.

It served him right!

Shortly after that incident I arrived home after work to find another police car outside my quarter.

I wondered whether the local farmer had made another complaint, and went indoors prepared to be belligerent, but it was nothing to do with that.

A bucolic looking, heavily built police sergeant and a petite brunette police woman were drinking tea at the dining table with my wife, and stood up as I entered.

I told them to sit again, and they explained why they were there.

A flasher had been showing off his goods in the field opposite Edith Weston primary school, which my daughter, Sheron, attended, and she had seen him.

They were worried about the effect it might have had on her, and wanted to question her about it.

My wife had insisted that they wait until I returned from work.

She had sent Sheron to play with her toys in the bedroom, but now that I was home she fetched her, and with great delicacy the police woman questioned her.

Yes, Sheron said, she had seen the man.

'Did he have something in his hand?' The police woman asked.

Yes, something that hung down, my daughter told her.

'Was it big?'

'Not very.'

She seemed not in the least bothered.

'He was there yesterday too, and lots of us saw him.' She added.

The two officers exchanged glances. That fact they had been unaware of.

'Can you tell us what he looks like?' The policewoman asked.

'He's old and he's got a little blue car.' Sheron said.

The male officer grunted, 'Charles.'

The police woman nodded her agreement.

Jacquie asked if they still needed Sheron, and was told no. She sent her back to play.

The policeman said, 'We know exactly who it was and where he lives. He's a regular client of ours, and when we tell him he was seen he will own up. We'll be off now to arrest him. Sheron seems to be well adjusted and does not think anything of the incident, but if she does suffer any trauma, please let us know.'

It was obvious that she hadn't been affected. I think the kids had just seen it as foolishness on the part of the old man, almost as if he were playing a game, for which we were very pleased.

Though his act was a terrible one, he was obviously not quite right in the head, doing what he did repeatedly in a place where it was a certainty that he would be caught. I was incensed that my daughter had been one of his 'victims' and would have been inclined to beat him to a pulp if I met him, but nevertheless, deep down, I believed that help to cure his compulsion in a psychiatric ward would in his case be more effective than prison.

It was not the kind of thing one expected to come across in that quiet, rural community.

I followed the case in the paper. He was sent to prison for six months, and I guess was not treated too well by the other prisoners, who would not be well disposed towards guys who flashed at small children.

Shortly after that I received a communication from London University, stating that I had been accepted as a candidate for an Honours Degree in German, with French as a subsidiary subject.

The length of study time was a mandatory five years – two years longer than the period spent by those actually attending the University, and the Degree Examination in French would be taken after three years.

There was also a note that a five-day Degree French course would be run during the Easter holiday for the Third Year students coming up to their Finals, and that I could attend that course if I paid a fee.

I leapt at the chance, and immediately sent the money off.

If I had not done that I might just have taken a different road in life when I came to another crossroads a week after sending off that money.

A knock came at the door and I answered it to find a smiling gentleman I did not recognise on the doorstep.

He was well dressed in a hand-stitched, light brown worsted suit and wore a military style tie.

I recognised immediately that he was someone who wanted to sell me something and was about to tell him that we did not do business at the door, but was somewhat intrigued when he introduced himself and handed me a card with his name on it and the fact that he was a life assurance representative.

I told him straight out that I was not interested, since I was an insurance agent myself and already had a life policy.

It was his turn to look intrigued.

The long and the short of it was that we were soon sitting at the kitchen table drinking tea and swapping stories.

He asked if I would be willing to give him my assessment of his selling method, which he had designed himself and which he thought '*did the business*'.

I agreed to do so, and he brought out from his briefcase a small pamphlet; a colourful little book with only ten pages.

He suggested, 'Go through it and fill in the boxes, Tony. I shall say nothing while you do so.'

I opened the booklet and began. The questions were regarding how much one could afford to pay, how much one imagined one would need at retirement age and so on.

They were so cleverly contrived that when one reached the last page, there was incontrovertible proof that one needed a policy and how much that policy should be for.

I was stunned. I looked up at him and said, 'This is incredible. The client sells himself the policy.'

He nodded, smiling, 'I thought you would like it. Now try to sell me a policy using the booklet.

I did so. It was so easy that the necessary questions came automatically.

When I had finished he leant his head on one side and looked at me thoughtfully before telling me, 'I have asked more than a dozen officers up to Wing Commander rank to assess that booklet, and not one of them has been able to do what you just did. You are a natural. How long have you still got to serve in the RAF?'

I told him, and just as Don MacLennon had done in Southern Rhodesia, he offered to buy me out of the RAF if I would join him in his enterprise. He earned, he told me, over twenty thousand pounds a year already and expected his income to top a hundred thousand within the next five years.

My annual pay at the time was just over one thousand.

It would entail two years 'on the road', visiting every Army and RAF camp in England, since he sold only to military personnel; another very clever part of his strategy – servicemen being assured of their continued employment in a world where other occupations were subject to sudden disasters.

After those two years, I would be based in the office and be able, he assured me, to 'write my own ticket'. He promised to make me a full partner at the end of those two years, on the same salary as his own, and would give me that assurance in writing, and witnessed by a solicitor, if I would join him.

I certainly considered the proposal seriously and called my wife in to discuss it, but finally decided to turn it down for one reason only: two years '*on the road*' was something I would hate. The RAF was an itinerant enough life, with its regular moves, and I wanted to lay down roots when I left it and have time to garden, shoot and fish.

It was a fabulous offer, and had I taken it I would now be worth tens of millions, because that man's company, ten years later, was one of the top five in the country, his name a household word, and I read in the paper how much he had sold it for when he was bought out.

Would I have enjoyed life any more if I had chosen that path? Who knows? I have enjoyed the life I have had as much as any man, and great wealth does not necessarily mean great happiness. Sufficiency is enough.

He accepted the decision, but left the offer open, should I change my mind during the following twelve months.

I did not.

The shooting around the airfield continued to be great, and I had to buy a second-hand ice-cream freezer to house the birds. At that time, only one household in a hundred had a freezer. It was quickly full, with almost a hundred pheasants in it, and I soon needed to buy a second one for vegetables.

I had longed for a garden throughout my service, and now had a large one behind the quarter and took on two large allotments in addition.

I really got the bug and went into gardening with a vengeance, as I did everything I was ever interested in. One good friend was correct when he described me as 'a shit or bust character'.

Had anyone seen the three walls around my telephone when I was ringing in to 'Millionaire', where one had to answer a question in twenty seconds in order to be considered for the show, they would have been convinced of that description.

Those walls were covered floor to ceiling with just about every fact known to man, from the height of every mountain in the world in feet and metres to the number of Ford Capris built in each year of production.

I rang every evening at least five times for over two years and was only shortlisted three times. The first time, after answering one question correctly, I was asked a subsidiary one, "What is the area of Sierra Leone in square kilometres?"

Something every kid on the block would know!

You can see the reason for the lists.

That is how I have always tackled anything: shit or bust.

With every vegetable in the ground that could be grown successfully in the UK, and a few that were decidedly doubtful, I started to grow exhibition chrysanthemums and dahlias, and the following year was exhibiting the football-sized blooms and winning prizes. Because of the conditions in Rutland, every bloom had to be covered with brown paper bags, to avoid damage by earwigs and the weather.

The prizes for those were not the only ones I was winning.

I'd joined a local rally club, and met there a man with the same surname, who liked navigating, Johnny Nash, an RAF sergeant in the electrical trade group.

We got on famously from the start and made up a team.

Everyone on the rally circuit thought we were brothers, and we had fun hamming it up.

Johnny's wife, Vicky, was as supporting of his involvement as my own.

We were two lucky fellows.

He had a contact in the RAF motor sport department, which had two Mini Cooper S vehicles, and soon we had our choice of them to rally with instead of my own vehicle, which was somewhat large for the job.

After winning a few rallies and talking to other drivers in the club who held International licences, I wanted to up my game, and applied to the Royal Automobile Club for a competition licence authorised by the Fédération Internationale de l'Automobile, so that we could enter the national RAC rallies.

Strangely enough, I came across that licence only three days ago, when clearing some rubbish out of my study, and have it in front of me as I write: it is No.FIA 65:2334.

The attached photograph shows a smart young fellow in RAF uniform, smiling at the camera. I don't recognise myself!

Having competed in two large rallies and done well, although not winning, I was contacted first by a representative of the Rootes Group, which made the Hillman Imp, and then by another rep from the Peugeot organisation, both of whom wanted us to rally their cars. They offered to pay all expenses, including hotel accommodation and meals, entry fees and fuel.

What was not to like?

Of course, I agreed.

The first time we used one of their cars it was a Hillman Imp, which they assured me had been prepared to top specification.

It had been, but unfortunately it had been Stage Three tuned for racing and sounded as if it had no baffles in the exhaust.

The rally was the RAC-sponsored *"Three Rivers Rally"*.

Penalties in the rally were, as usual, for lost time - a point a minute, but one 'fault' was worse than all the minutes one could possibly accumulate.

At the start, one of the adjudicators came up to the window and asked me to rev the engine, so that he could check the level of sound produced.

I did so. The noise would have awakened the dead.

He winced as the needle on his device tried to wrap itself round the end stop.

'Just a minute,' he urged, 'I'll walk away a bit, and then try again.'

He trotted about fifty yards away and wiggled his finger for me to blip the throttle again.

I did so, for only a fraction of a second, and again he winced.

He strolled back and said, 'Just let the engine tick over.'

He watched the dial and then told us sorrowfully, 'Sorry, chaps, even on idle it's reading a hundred and ten decibels. I'll have to give you a fault.'

At that point we might just as well have gone home, but we were at the start so decided to go through with it.

We did very well, only losing thirty-one minutes in time, which would have put us in the top ten, but were given another fault at the half-way stage and yet another at the end. Three faults – it could not possibly have been worse.

Once bitten! It was the last time we used a Hillman, although the Rootes Group guy kept at us to do so. The Imp might be okay on a normal road, but I didn't like the handling on a rally.

We used works Peugeots for all large rallies after that, on one of which I had the pleasure of driving down a river bed, with water up to the door sills, near the top of Betws y Coed at midnight in a heavy snowstorm, a delight any rally driver would happily give up a night's sleep for!

We must have been doing something right, because it was shortly after that when I was selected by the company to drive a 404 in the East African Safari.

I was overjoyed, and applied for special leave from the RAF to take part.

It was granted, and my excitement grew as the date came closer.

Then, for some inexplicable reason, the special leave was cancelled.

I did not have enough annual leave left to cover the three weeks the team would be away, so with heavy heart had to cancel my involvement.

As it happened, the second driver wrote the car off on the first day of the rally, by ripping the sump off on a huge boulder in a dry river bed, and that was the end of its involvement, but oh, how I would have longed to be there! Maybe I would have been driving instead of the other guy, and maybe....

I rallied for fourteen years, losing scores of night's sleep, and that in itself is a story.

I like to say that though I have over-indulged in everything in life, smoking over a hundred Capstan Full Strength cigarettes a day for fourteen years until I woke one day and coughed up a pint and a half of blood – not the best way of giving up, but bloody effective, and being a borderline alcoholic all my life, I have never taken drugs, but that is not entirely true.

Throughout the entire time I rallied I was given pills by various RAF doctors without question to get me through those nights without sleep – the same pills they had given the aircrews flying over Germany during the war, and they issued them to us without a qualm, a hundred at a time. They were, of course, the amphetamine Dexadrin, which is now a controlled substance.

I never felt any side effects, not even noticing the euphoria they are supposed to bring on, and they were pretty marvellous in doing the job we took them for – to stay awake.

We averaged two rallies a month, and almost all of them entailed leaving home after tea on a Friday to drive anything up to two hundred miles to the start, then, after completing the entry forms and going through the vehicle checks, rallying for probably another two hundred miles, after which we would wait for the results and then drive home, usually arriving some time on Sunday morning or afternoon. Those pills were highly necessary.

It was no wonder we enjoyed our rallying. We must have been as high as kites!

CHAPTER THIRTEEN

Easter arrived, and I took myself off to London by train for the Vacation course in French, staying at the Union Jack Club by Waterloo Station, the subsidised Forces club.

I reported early on the first day of the course and was shown to an empty auditorium, with banks of seats going up from low at the front to very high at the back.

I climbed up to the highest row, intending to keep as low a profile as possible, and a while later the place filled up, with about a hundred and fifty students sat below and around me.

The course was run by the professor who headed the Modern Languages Department of the University, Doctor Landers.

He was a terrific teacher, and at the end of the second two-hour session after lunch, handed out papers for translation into French as homework.

The next day they were collected and another translation given out.

At the start of the session on the third day he went through some of the 'clangers' that had been dropped by various students in their translations, and began a rant about one particular facet, which almost everyone had got wrong.

'It seems,' he pointed out, 'that hardly any of you know the 'GE' gender rule. Is there anyone in the auditorium who can tell me what it is?'

I knew it, but was not about to call attention to myself, being sure that someone else would know.

Nevertheless, I lifted a finger, hidden from view by the head of the student in front of me.

Doctor Landers glanced around.

'I thought not, and you people are intending to go out there and teach others the language. Not one of you has bothered to learn it! That is terrible! Is there no one who knows?'

I thought, why not, and lifted my arm.

He peered upwards as if he could not believe his eyes and asked, 'Do you want to leave the room or do you really know the answer?'

'I know the answer, sir.' I told him.

'And what is it?'

'All nouns ending in 'GE' are masculine, except for CAGE, PAGE, PLAGE, NAGE, RAGE and IMAGE.'

He glared around at the other students. 'Now *that* is what I expect from all of you! That man deserves success.' He looked up at me again and said, 'I don't recognise you. Please stay behind afterwards. I would like to talk to you.'

When the others had trooped out and I descended from my lofty perch and introduced myself, giving him my history, he congratulated me again on my dedication and told me that if I ever needed a recommendation I should contact him. My translation, he said, was grade A.

I was to meet him again after my Finals, when he laughed and said that I was only the second student he had ever known – the previous one being a Pole – who had memorised a huge chunk of French literary history from the Lagarde et Michard manual –

the French literary student's Bible when it came to learning about any French writer or period of French literary history, which had obtained for me the top mark available for that paper.

Because of my difficulty in knowing how to prepare for the examination papers, I studied carefully the questions from the previous ten years' papers, and found that every second or third year there was a question about the so-called 'rules' of French seventeenth century literature, which entailed unity of time, place and manner.

The questions had to be answered in French, of course, and so I learnt off by heart a huge chunk of the book which dealt with those rules.

Then, I practised writing it, over and over again, to make sure that I could get it down on paper in the hour allowed.

With practice, I managed it in fifty-five minutes.

I can remember it today and could still write it in full. It began: *"Ces fameuses règles, centre de controverse pendant des siècles....*

I had spent hundreds of hours on the French set books, which included eighteenth and nineteeth century poetry, and became enchanted with some of it; particularly that of Paul Verlaine, a Symbolist poet, whose evocative poems made one feel almost a part of them. I often still find parts of them arriving out of nowhere in my brain.

Whether it was because of my rally driving or not I don't know, but I had been at North Luffenham less than a week when I was asked by the unit CO if I would be willing to drive the courier to London every Friday.

The job I had been given was not demanding, and I seized the chance to have a day on the road once a week instead of sitting in the office, working out, as we had to, the Difficulty Factor and Difficulty Value of each question we were using in both the examinations we were setting and those that had been sat, in order to make future ones equivalent in standard.

The courier was usually the same Flight Lieutenant, who had the courier bag chained and locked to his wrist, and we soon got onto first name terms. The car we used was one of the sit-up-and-beg, standard RAF Minis, a far cry from the Cooper-S I had been driving in rallies, with a performance that included a nought-to-sixty time of about half a day and a top speed of sixty-eight, but it did the job after a fashion and got us there and back all right.

After doing the run for just over a year, we almost came to a sticky end.

We'd reached the outskirts of the Metropolis and had just gone over the brow of a hill in Shoreditch when I saw a woman with a pram, waiting to cross the road at a marked pedestrian crossing, about eighty yards down the hill.

I braked to a halt to allow her to cross and suddenly saw her look to her right in fright, her eyes wide and her mouth open.

My eyes flew to the rear view mirror, and I saw a large white lorry, which had obviously been exceeding the speed limit, skidding almost sideways down the steep hill behind us.

It was quite clear that it was going to crash into us.

I shouted, 'Brace yourself, Jim!' and pushed my hands hard against th dashboard.

There were no safety belts fitted in the car, and, of course, it was way before air bags had been invented.

The lorry slammed into the back of the Mini, pushing us more than forty yards over the crossing.

Had the woman stepped off the pavement, we would have killed her and the baby.

I was incensed, but had my wits about me.

The engine was still running, and I switched off the ignition and set the hand brake.

After asking the courier if he was all right and having been shakily told, 'I think so', I urged, 'Give me a pen.'

Without asking why, he took one from his pocket and passed it to me.

I tore the blank bottom half off one of the travel documents, wrote a sentence on it, jumped out of the car and strode purposefully up to the door of the lorry and pulled it open.

I won't repeat what I said to the driver, but it was highly colourful, and he nodded in agreement.

He looked dazed and kept repeating, 'I'm sorry.'

'So you bloody should be!' I stormed. 'Sign this!'

I thrust the pen and paper at him.

He glanced at what I had written and without ado signed underneath it.

'Give me your insurance docs.' I demanded, and he fudged around in the glove compartment, found them and passed them over.

I wrote down the company, the policy number and the registration number of the van and handed them back.

'What's your name?'

He told me and I wrote that down too.

I blurted, 'You could have fucking killed us, and that woman and baby, you stupid bastard.'

He nodded, 'I know, mate. I'm so sorry.'

'You bloody will be!' I told him and turned on my heel.

The woman, still looking blanched, had been waiting, talking to Jim.

I got her to make a written statement too and told her to go on her way.

The luck, and the gods, had been on her side that day.

It was horrifically different when almost the exact scenario was played out again in front of my eyes over thirty years later.

I had stopped when the traffic light at a pedestrian crossing in front of me changed to red.

From the other direction I was horrified to see a Vauxhall Astra hurtling up the road towards the crossing, travelling at way over the thirty miles per hour limit.

I flashed my headlights, but the driver was looking out to the side, not forwards.

Before I could sound my horn or turn the window down to warn the pedestrian, a fifteen-year old girl, she stepped off the pavement.

The Vauxhall smashed headlong into her body, throwing it ten feet into the air.

She landed on her head, and I saw her neck snap backwards.

She died instantly.

The Vauxhall had gone more than fifty yards before it stopped, and I saw the reversing lights come on. He was preparing for the investigation.

I gave evidence, stating clearly that the traffic light had been red, both to the police and at the inquest.

The other driver, a man of twenty, whose girlfriend, I found out, would not even ride in a car with him, because he was such a lunatic at the wheel, had insisted that the light on his side was on green. He was backed up by the driver of the car behind him, which had also gone over the crossing before stopping. He found another 'witness', obviously a friend, who had not given evidence to the police on the day of the accident, he said, because he had 'not wanted to get involved', but 'came forward to see that an injustice was not done', stating that he had been walking along further back on the pavement and clearly saw that the Vauxhall had gone over a green light, not a red one.

The inspector in charge of the case told me they knew perfectly well that what I had told them was right, but could not prove it. He told me the killer already had two convictions for driving without due care and attention, as well as speeding offences.

The driver of the Vauxhall, instantly recognising what he had done, had not braked hard enough to leave skid marks on the road and had backed up to where the body lay, making it appear that he had not been speeding.

To add insult to injury, at the Coroner's inquest, I was berated by the old boy for giving false evidence. It was obvious that I was wrong, he insisted quite angrily, since the other two witnesses' stories matched exactly. I had wasted the court's time and should be ashamed of myself.

I wanted to scream at him, and had difficulty holding my anger in, but knew I was on a hiding to nothing if I let fly in his courtroom.

That driver, who had turned and was smirking at me, having deliberately perverted the course of justice and got away with it, had committed murder – plain and simple.

~~~oOo~~~

Jim and I inspected the damage.

From the front it was obvious that the entire body of the Mini was skewed. The back wheels were out of alignment with the front by about three inches.

The back of the car was crushed in completely, but surprisingly nowhere near as badly as I had expected. The monocoque design had taken the huge blow well, although the sub-frame had suffered.

The back window was smashed, as were the two rear side windows, and the back seat and foot wells were covered in tiny shards of glass, but the rear wheels had no metal pushed in on them to stop them turning.

Looking at it, I wondered it if was drivable.

I asked Jim, 'What do you think? Shall I give it a go?'

He shrugged, 'I could find a telephone and have them send out a vehicle.'

I could see by the way he was clutching his courier briefcase that it was the very last thing he wanted to do. He'd obviously seen some of the same spy films that I had, where an accident was staged so that the bad guys could steal the briefcase from the courier by chopping off his hand, and he was worried about his vulnerability even more than the state of the Mini.

I suggested, 'Get in, and we'll see if she'll go.'

He did, and I slid onto the driver's seat.

The Mini started without any trouble, and I went through the gears with my foot on the clutch. They all seemed to work. I drove a few feet and tried the brakes. We stopped all right.

I was satisfied that it would get us to our destination safely, but took it very easily.

It was akin to driving a drunken pig, and I could clearly feel it crabbing along, no doubt ripping chunks of rubber off the tread of the tyres, but we got there and parked up.

Jim, obviously relieved that he had got his top secret papers there safely, disappeared inside after assuring me that he would arrange a replacement vehicle to get us back to North Luffenham.

He was surprisingly quick.

When he came out, he was accompanied by another officer, a baby-faced, blond haired Flight Lieutenant, who took one look at the Mini and pronounced, 'That's a write-off.'

As if we didn't know that.

We were both extremely lucky that we had not suffered whip-lash injuries.

Despite that, had it been the present day, we would have been involved in litigation, looking for four-figure sums in compensation, like everyone else.

In those days, one would just grin and bear it.

I expected that we would be given rail warrants and have to make our own way back, but the Flight Louie quickly arranged for a car and driver, and we were chauffeured back in style in a luxurious Rover P6 executive saloon.

The next day I reported to the motor transport section to tell the MT officer that he had better order a replacement for one written-off Mini.

He looked at me with compassion.

'You know you are going to be filling in forms from now until Doomsday, don't you?'

I grinned at him, 'Will this do?'

I handed him the bit of paper I'd got the lorry driver to sign.

It included details of place, time, vehicle registration numbers and names and stated that he admitted that the accident was entirely his fault and that he had caused it by exceeding the speed limit and therefore was unable to brake in time to stop hitting our vehicle, which was stopped at a pedestrian crossing.

The MT officer looked up at me and shook his head.

'You are a jammy bugger.'

'No, sir. A driver with foresight.'

He nodded, 'That too. Okay, you can forget the paperwork. You will not hear another thing about it.'

I threw him off a salute and he gave me one back, grinning as he said, 'You are still a jammy bugger.'

'Yes, sir.' I told him, grinning just as widely.

During my lifetime, I have been involved in four accidents, none of which have been my fault, and in all but one of those instances, in which, quite wrongly, as it turned out, I considered it completely unnecessary, I have had the other driver sign a statement of liability. My NCB has never been in question.

## CHAPTER FOURTEEN

We had few parades at North Luffenham, but on one of them I and two other SNCOs were called out for a medal to be pinned on each of our chests.

I was now an officially recognised decorated veteran!

The medal was the Long Service and Good Conduct Medal, awarded for eighteen years of meritorious service, better known, and probably more accurately, to all and sundry as the 'gong' one received for 'Eighteen Years of Undetected Crime'.

Study for the Honours Degree was a must, and I was putting in a lot of hours a week on the set books, but for two of the papers, Old High German and Middle High German, I could find no help.

Nottingham University was not very far away, and I wrote to the Head of the German Department, asking if there was any literature they could suggest that might help me.

I received a very nice letter back from the Professor in charge of that Department, Professor Yuile, offering to allow me to attend on a part-time basis his courses in those two subjects, in which I would join his third year students for the final three months of their study before their Finals. It was on Thursday afternoons.

That was a predicament. How could I ask for the time off? Then I had an idea.

I put in a general application to be allowed to attend Nottingham University on games afternoons.

It was approved, and I drove over to meet the Professor, after telephoning to make an appointment.

He agreed the arrangement, and I duly began to attend the classes.

It was extremely hard work to begin with: Old High German was as different to Modern German as Old Saxon is to Modern English – a completely different language!

In fact, I was surprised to learn that Old Saxon, from which our modern speech is derived, was written almost identically and therefore must have been spoken identically, to Old High German.

The Professor pointed this out by showing us excerpts from Bishop Wulfila's 4th Century Old Saxon and Old High German Bibles, one quote from Genesis of which I remember: *"Wellagu nu, thu Ewa, quath Atham..."* was the Saxon, and *"Uuelagu nu, đu Euua, quađ Ađam..."* the Old High German.

Not much difference at all, apart from the double 'u', which, I guess, is where we got our word for that letter from.

Of course, only the monks could write, and how they wrote depended on which monastery they lived in. Even the Bishop's name was sometimes written as 'Ulfilas'.

Middle High German has slightly more mental clicks with the modern language, but is still far removed from it.

I struggled, sitting at the back, aware that the guys and gals in front of me had done almost three years study of the subjects.

After seven or eight weeks I found them asking if they could look at my homework before the sessions began, and was amazed when they asked if they could copy it.

It was unbelievable. After only a couple of months I was ahead of them!

One afternoon, Professor Yuile asked me to stay behind. He wanted to congratulate me on my fast progress.

I told him it had been hard, but was coming on nicely. In fact it had stimulated in me a desire to know much more about semantics and comparative linguistics.

I couldn't help telling him my opinion of the other students, and he sighed and nodded.

'You are absolutely right,' he said, 'some of them are real dunces, and I worry that we are about to send them out into the big wide world to be teachers, when they are not up to scratch.'

'But why,' I asked, 'do you have to give them their degrees? Can't you fail them?'

He sighed again and told me, 'If they have managed to last out to the third year we have to pass them. There was one chap who had been the Student Representative since he began here, a real Red under the bed, who we had to re-class four times, and he was still so bad at the end that the University had to create a 'Pass' grade for the Honours Course, just to cater for him. We couldn't fail him.

'But that's awful,' I said, 'and surely is a contradiction in terms.'

He smiled grimly and nodded, 'Exactly.'

Many years later, I was engaged to do a job for the University of East Anglia and had to liaise with the Student Representative, since it involved student accommodation.

I turned up at the University at around ten-thirty in the morning and asked to see him.

The girl undergraduate manning the desk in the Student Centre looked shocked, 'You won't be able to see him till this afternoon.' She insisted.

'Why?' I asked, 'Is he in lectures until then?'

'Oh, no.' She told me, as if it was the most natural thing in the world, 'He never gets up until at least two o'clock.'

He was another one who would wind up with a degree he did not deserve!

Near the end of the course I asked the Prof if he would allow me to attend his course during the next term, and he agreed immediately, but told me it would be on a different day, not Thursday.

That put the kibosh on it. The RAF would certainly not go for that, and I told him so.

He then said that if I ever needed help with any difficulty I should contact him.

I thanked him for the offer, but knew I could never take him up on it.

After the last lesson before his students took their examinations, I thanked him again sincerely, and he said that he had been impressed with my dedication and that if I ever wanted a job reference I should contact him, as Doctor Landers had done.

A very nice gentleman.

Shortly after that I sat the French Degree examination and passed it. One great hurdle behind me. Now I could concentrate on the German, and all those books!

Looking back, I just can't fathom how I managed to fit it all in: my work, the rallying for a whole weekend at least twice a month, the two allotments and garden, the flower care and exhibitions, the shooting, and, of course, the matter of being a husband and father. I'd also taken up Provincial French and Middle Eastern cuisine, and was becoming quite adept at producing authentic dishes from both areas.

Something had to give, and it was my stomach. I was diagnosed as having a huge ulcer! It was painful, but didn't hold me back.

I wanted another tour overseas, preferably in Germany, to help with my studies, and applied once more for a posting there.

It was approved, and I began to make preparations to move.

I decided that the next rally would be the last. It was a two-hundred-and-seventy mile event, with special forest stages and speed sections.

We came seventh of sixty-eight entries and drove home tired but satisfied.

I had driven over a hundred thousand rally miles and had never so much as scratched one of the cars I had driven.

The posting came through.

I was going back to Gatow, this time as a senior Flight Sergeant. I had checked, as one could in those days, and found that I was top of the promotion roster to Warrant Officer, but with the cutbacks there had been no such promotion in my trade for the last four years, and there would be no more until well after I left the RAF.

Shortly before the due date, we handed over the quarter, and my wife moved back to Norfolk with our daughter, to live with her mother and father until we were allocated a quarter in Berlin.

Another Flight Sergeant was keen on taking over the allotments, and I happily let him have the vegetables that were growing there.

It was the end of an enjoyable chapter of my life, and I was ready for the next one.

Gerry and I had a last pint together the evening before I left.

He came back to Norfolk to live after his service, and we have met up a few times over the years, but since he lived thirty miles away we never shot together again.

I shed tears when he rang me up at Christmas a couple of months ago and told me stoically that he had been given at the most three weeks to live. What had been treated for five years as diverticulitis was actually cancer, and they had caught it too late.

He died just after the festive season.

CHAPTER FIFTEEN

I had been informed when applying for a ПУТЕВКА for the trip through the East Zone that I should arrive at Checkpoint Bravo no later than eleven in the morning, in time to join the escort vehicle, so instead of attempting to drive the six hundred miles to Berlin in one go, after crossing from Dover to Calais, I did it the easy way and stayed one night at a hotel in Cologne and another in Wolfsburg, close to the border.

Driving in the opposite direction to that in which I'd last done the trip was far easier; for some reason the Russians appeared to mind less us travelling *to* Berlin than from it, and the check was much shorter in duration at the Helmstedt end and almost a wave-through at the other.

As I drove in through the gate at Gatow it felt like coming home, and I was soon back in the swing of things, looking forward to shooting the rabbits, of which there seemed hundreds all over the place, as soon as I had my wife with me and our own place to cook them. Both the air rifle and the twelve-bore had accompanied me on the trip.

The arrival formalities included a briefing about 'Exercise Rocking Horse' – something new since my last posting there, an exercise that for some reason was always carried out in the middle hours of the night.

It was the stand-to of all personnel not already on duty, and was an exercise intended to make us ready to stop the invaders if the Ruskis ever decided to roll in and take over the three western sectors of the city.

It was utterly ludicrous.

How we were supposed to stop the massed squadrons of tanks they would use with just a couple of Lee Enfields – not everybody had one - was anybody's guess, but it must have made someone in the higher echelons happy that a token defence would be made.

I could have told them they had absolutely no reason to worry – the mere sight of me with my trusty .177 air rifle standing in his path would have scared the pants off any armoured column commander and sent him scurrying back to his barracks.

It was just as well I had been briefed, because at three-fifteen the next morning I was brought out of a deep sleep by the noise of all the sirens on camp, whistles, and oft-repeated, ear-splitting loudspeaker announcements: *"EXERCISE ROCKING HORSE, EXERCISE ROCKING HORSE, EXERCISE ROCKING HORSE"* coming from the vehicles fitted with audio equipment that were driving around the camp.

There were many moans and groans from the sleepy-eyed airmen I joined at my appointed post.

There we stood, after a roll call had been taken, like spare pricks at a lesbian wedding, for almost half an hour, before the vehicles drove round again, announcing the end of the exercise.

It was to recur almost once a month for the whole of my tour.

After applying for a quarter, I sent in the usual application for permission to shoot on the camp and was interviewed by the adjutant.

When I'd given him details of my experience, including the fact that I had shot on my last posting to Gatow, he gave permission, but made a point that 'under no circumstances was I to shoot the deer'. It would offend the Germans too much, he said.

Tongue in cheek and with fingers firmly crossed, I assured him that I would abide by that decision.

He then asked if I would like to take over the rifle club; something I had not intended to do this time, and he seemed keen that I should do so.

It was no skin off my back, and I agreed. The availability .22 rifles might come in handy.

When it came to handover I found out why he was so keen: he had been lumbered with its safe-keeping and wanted to off-load it.

The set room in Hanbury Block looked exactly the same as when I had left it, and my first job was NCO i/c – a day job.

The watch system was the same as it had always been, two on, two off, morning and evening the first day and afternoon and night the next, with a sleeping day, followed by a free day, before the two working days began again.

The lads were a good bunch, and hard workers, but, human nature being what it is, liked to 'get their heads down' on night duty, and on checking I found that intercepts for the night hours were way down on what they should have been.

I began to visit the section at all hours of the night, sometimes early on, around one or two o'clock, and sometimes later, around five or six – that dreadful period in a watch when even the most dedicated of operators begin to droop.

Every time I would be assured that there was 'nothing doing, Flight', at which time I would sit down at each position in turn and begin twiddling the dial.

By the time I left, every operator in the room would be logging one of his required groups.

I had not long been back when I overheard a conversation that concerned me and learnt that I had acquired a new nickname: *"The Old Slavedriver"*.

It stayed with me until I left the unit, and I felt quite proud of the name. It proved that I was successful in the job that I was doing.

During my service and since, whenever I have employed men, I have always made sure that I could do each of their jobs faster and more efficiently that they could, and would not hesitate to take on the dirtiest, some of which were so disgusting that I would not want to describe them here.

Not long after my arrival, I was for some obtuse reason selected as one of the six men who would greet Harold Wilson when he landed at Gatow for his visit with the Mayor of Berlin, Willy Brandt.

I had hated the Labour Party since they made the devastating cuts to the RAF that had cut short my flying career, and Wilson himself I believed to be one of the most devious prime ministers we had ever had. He could certainly not count me among his fans.

The 'big' day arrived, and he descended from the aircraft and shook hands with us.

I wrote a letter to my parents, who held the same opinions of the man as I did, and wrote the first page shakily with my left hand, ending with: "I am having to write this with my left hand, since my right has had to be amputated."

At the top of the next page, in my normal script, I wrote, "Because I was forced to shake hands with Harold Wilson".

It was supposed to be funny, but my mother, so my father told me angrily, almost fainted when she read it, and didn't read the second page. My weird sense of humour had got me into trouble yet again.

There were no opportunities to rally in the city, of course, but my time was full up. I studied every spare minute, began selling insurance again, bought and sold a couple of ex-American Army cars, took dozens of pictures and did some shooting and sailing on the Havel, having re-joined the Yacht Club.

I made a bad mistake early one Sunday morning, driving along Klosterstrasse, in the Mitte district, by not following my instincts when involved in an accident.

It was very early, and the street was empty of traffic.

I saw a heavily built man come out of a house about two hundred yards ahead of me and get into a Volkswagen beetle.

A puff of exhaust told me he had started the engine, and I flashed my lights to let him know I was moving towards him.

Without any warning, he pulled out, just as my front bumper was coming level with his rear one.

I leant on the horn and frantically yanked the wheel over to try to avoid his vehicle, which I would have achieved, except that the other driver had not pulled out to drive straight on, but intended crossing the road to enter the side road on the opposite side.

It is a three-lane road, the surface on that day wet cobbles, with tram tracks in the middle lane, and we finally made contact in the third lane, right on the other side of the road, since I had the choice of going over the pavement to hit a house or having a minor crunch with the VW.

It was the lesser of the two evils.

The crash was unavoidable. My car had a bent right wing and his VW had a bent rear one.

I got out and began to give him a piece of my mind.

Somehow, the jungle telegraph worked, and a German police car arrived, with a sergeant and a constable as crew.

The sergeant listened to my story, and the German driver, a Herr Wollschendorf, agreed it in every particular.

He stated, 'I thought the road was empty. I didn't see the English car, so pulled out to cross the road.'

The sergeant checked, 'So, Herr Wollschendorf, you are admitting that the accident was entirely your fault?'

There was slight hesitation, and I could see the other driver didn't want to agree, but he finally grunted, 'Ja'.

The policeman wrote it all down in his little book and told me, 'Go and get your vehicle repaired. This man's insurance will pay.'

I asked, 'Can I just take a signed statement from him?'

'Absolutely unnecessary.' He insisted, 'He has admitted being solely at fault and we have his statement written down.'

I had the car repaired and took the bill to his insurance company.

After much to-ing and fro-ing, and whispered conversations between clerks, one of them told me, 'You must be wrong. Herr Wollschendorf has not been involved in an accident.'

Imagine my indignation. I exclaimed, 'He damned well has, and here is the proof!'

They took the matter up, and a few days later I received a letter from them which stated, 'Herr Wollschendorf has now informed us of the accident, but claims that you were entirely responsible for it. He is the innocent party.

A statement from him was enclosed, which, after giving details of the date and time, read, 'I was driving along Klosterstrasse when I was overtaken by a speeding British car, which suddenly veered right and struck my vehicle. I believe the other driver to have been drunk.'

I hit the roof.

Back at the insurance company I ranted and raved, but they were adamant: they were taking their stance according to what they had been told.

I pointed out that the police had told me they would pay, because the other driver was totally at fault.

They then showed me a letter from the police, which stated that it had been impossible, due to conflicting accounts by the two drivers, to determine who had been at fault.

Wollschendorf was a cheeky bastard. He wrote to my Commanding Officer, demanding that the cost of his car repairs be deducted from my pay.

When I explained to the CO what had happened, he sent a beautifully worded reply, telling Wollschendorf in no uncertain terms to 'get stuffed'.

He also made an appointment for me to see the top barrister we employed at the Stadium.

When I had given the legal gentleman the facts, he told me sadly, 'It grieves me to have to say this, since I am German also, but our police are not incorruptible. This police sergeant you spoke to has taken a large bribe from the other driver and destroyed the notes taken at the scene. I am afraid that you will have to pay for your own damages.'

It was bad enough, but that was not the end of it.

Unbelievably, Wollschendorf turned up at the guardroom one day, with his two sons, and demanded to see me, to get payment for his repairs.

Being called from work, I raced down to the guardroom in my car and leapt out, nicely wound up and ready for anything.

Wollschendorf was standing beside his car with two younger men, both well built and over six feet tall. Two service policemen stood on the pavement nearby, expecting trouble.

The German looked a bit pooh-faced, but still began demanding payment for his repairs.

In his own language I told him at the top of my voice that he knew damned well that he alone had caused the accident and had admitted that fact to the police in my hearing. I lied and told him that our legal department at the Stadium had contacted the Internal Investigation department of the Berlin police force, with a view to charging the sergeant who had been at the scene and taken the statements, and him, with bribery and corruption.

It hit the right spot – he looked horrified.

I followed it up with, 'And if you don't get back right now into your little fart-box of a car and piss off and stop bothering me I am going to knock your and your two little woofters' teeth so far down your throats that you will have to stick your toothbrushes up your arses to clean them.'

The two six-footers seemed to shrink at least six inches.

From the looks they gave their father, I knew for sure that he had told them a pack of lies, and not the true facts.

One of them turned and opened the car door, and that caused the rot.

The three of them disappeared into the interior and shot off.

One of the SPs, who was married to a German girl and had learnt some of the language asked, 'Did you just tell them what I thought you did? I heard the word for toothbrush and Arschloch.'

I nodded, 'If they'd stayed, you'd have had blood to clear up.'

Though now I write about murder in every conceivable way, I think that day I came as close to committing it as it is possible to get without actually carrying out the act.

Wollschendorf never tried it on again.

Since then, I always carry a pad of writing paper and a pen in every vehicle I drive, and have used it twice to good effect.

CHAPTER SIXTEEN

I had, on a couple of occasions, visited the pub in Kladow, *"Zum Dorfkrug"*, but Liese was no longer the Wirtin, and it just did not seem to have the same ambiance.

Keen to have the most help I could get with my studies, I visited Berlin University and asked the Chancellor's office if there was any possibility I could attend the odd lecture.

Certainly, they told me – I could apply for a 'Hörerkarte', which cost only a few marks.

I did so on the spot, paid the fee and received the card.

I duly applied for permission to attend on sports afternoon – something I had not been in the habit of taking off.

Permission was given, and then, before I could attend even one lecture, I was hauled in to see the adjutant again and told that under no circumstances was I to go anywhere near the University. It was, he said, a hotbed of Communism, and I was to disassociate myself from it immediately.

I tore up the Hörerkarte.

After only three months, a quarter in one of the new blocks was allocated to me, and normal married life resumed, except that our daughter was not with us.

In order that her schooling should not be disrupted by too much change, we had arranged for her to be a part-boarder at Wymondham College, only three miles away from my mother's bungalow, where she would spend weekends and holidays, except those she spent with us after flying out to Berlin.

At the time, it seemed like the very best solution to the problem, but it was not.

Many years later, she told us how desperately unhappy she had been the whole time she was away from us, and how it had so badly affected her schooling.

I took over the quarter and added a few extras, met my wife at Tempelhof and moved in with her.

I converted one of the bedrooms into a darkroom and went into photography big time again.

Soon I was taking the photographs at weddings and other 'dos', charging hardly anything for doing so, and then began doing artistic portraits, which in part was responsible for my move onto the downward path in the fidelity stakes.

I exhibited some of my wife in local competitions, winning prizes with them, and was approached by several of the other wives and some husbands, asking if I would do some for them.

One thing led to another, and the other was a request for me to take a nude portrait.

I kept that secret from my wife, but did it, and was very happy with the result, as was the woman who had sat for it.

Expecting it to be a one-off was naïve of me! The ladies' jungle telegraph worked too well for that to happen.

It was followed by others, and I began enjoying certain side benefits, which also must have gone onto that 'telegraph', considering the expansion of those particular delights.

It was at that time too that I learnt the true details of 'knickers, WAAF officers for the use of', referred to earlier.

It was another secret that could not possibly be kept – too many people knew about it - and one day I received a telephone call from the adjutant, asking me to drop in and see him.

He was obviously embarrassed and hedged around the point until he asked me to please stop doing portraits.

'*Of any kind*', was how he put it.

I was most unhappy about it – I had been enjoying myself immensely – but acceded to his request.

As it happened, it made no difference to the merry-go-round, except that a certain officer was quite suddenly and inexplicably posted to another unit in the British Zone.

When asked to do one lot of wedding photographs, of a sergeant to a local German girl, the groom asked me if I knew anyone who could translate the wedding ceremony into German - a legal requirement, he told me.

I said it would be no bother for me to do it, but there was a snag.

The translator had to be officially recognised as an interpreter/translator, and for that one needed to be registered with the Berlin Government.

I registered, did the translation, was paid the huge sum of fourteen marks – three pounds fifty - the set fee for a mundane translation being three Pfennigs a word, and forgot about it until I received a request to do another translation, this time from a chemical company in the city.

This time it was from German to English, but I had never heard of many of the highly technical and specialist words and expressions in either language.

It was all grist to the mill, of course, and could only help my linguistic skills, so I agreed, but this time at a rate of twenty Pfennigs a word.

I should have made it fifty! That translation took me most of a weekend, and was the first of many from that firm and others.

The largest translation I did was the Operating Instructions for Tegel Airport, from French into English and German, an entire booklet of over sixty pages.

I was asked to do the same translation as before for another wedding, for which I was paid, although I had kept a copy and had to do no work, but was also asked to attend as interpreter at the wedding, since the bride spoke no English.

Another first, but not the last.

Quite a number of much more interesting and demanding interpreting jobs came up, all of which I carried out, until, with the Degree Finals approaching, I had to stop, in order to concentrate on my studies.

I had to have some escape from them, and carried on with the shooting. Apart from anything else, it gave me an excuse for being away from the quarter when my wife was home from her work in the NAAFI shop at Summit Place, so that I could continue with the side benefits, but I did actually do some shooting.

There were five roe deer in one of the woods and two in another, and I had been watching them for some time, wondering how I could manage to poach one of them without the powers-that-be finding out.

I'd bought from a gun shop in Berlin some twelve-bore solid slugs, illegal in England, which some Germans used to shoot deer and wild boar.

They were normal looking cartridges, slightly longer than usual, and the slug was an inch-and-a-quarter long lump of rifled lead.

I had tried one out on a small tree with a circumference of around four inches and was horrified when the damned thing fell, its stem blown completely apart by the shot.

I dragged it out of sight and used some mud to plaster on the freshly scarred wood.

They would certainly bring a deer down, I knew.

One day, stalking carefully through the wood, I saw a deer, its head behind a bush, but with a clear shot at the vital area near the knuckle of the foreleg.

I took the shot and the deer disappeared, but came out the other side of the bush.

Believing that I had missed with the first shot I shot again, and the roe crumpled.

I quickly dragged it away, gralloched it and buried the gralloch, went back for my car and drove it home.

Just over a week later the adjutant sent for me again and demanded, 'Have you been shooting deer, Flight Sergeant?'

'Me, sir? No, sir? Why?' I hoped I looked as innocent as I sounded.

'There is a deer carcase', he told me, 'in the wood, with a large hole blown through its shoulder. Come with me.'

He drove me out to where I had shot the deer.

Behind the bush lay a carcase, eaten away by foxes, but quite obviously it had been shot, because the shoulder blade was smashed to pieces.

I had killed both deer, and it taught me a lesson I have never forgotten: never accept that you have missed a deer. Always check, and then check again!

After ten months i/c setroom, I was moved into the reporting section, where the emphasis was on maintaining full records of the radars operating over the whole of Russia and the Eastern Block.

There were three lads and myself.

It was new work for me and highly interesting. Up on the notice board at the top were the goals of ELINT:

*"To know the capabilities of the enemy's electronic equipment.*

*To work out the enemy's Order of Battle.*

*To develop electronic counter measures against the enemy's electronic equipment."*

We recorded the hours of activity of dozens of different radars, both land-based and airborne, the *"Tall King"*, *"Knife Rest"* and *"Spoon Rest"* early warning radars in places as far away as Tashkent, in Uzbekistan, and Omsk and Novosibirsk in Siberia, and similar radars with wonderful names like *"Bar Lock"*, *"Big Mesh" and "Dumbo"* at dozens of other different locations all over the target area.

The missile fire control and target acquisition radars of the many different surface-to-air missile systems the Ruskis used were less regularly intercepted, but there were hundreds of intercepts of such radars as the *"Fan Song"* of the SA-2 system, the *"Straight Flush"* of the SA-6, and the *"Tomb Stone"* and *"Grave Stone"* of the SA-20 and 21 systems, to name just six of the fifteen or so that they used. Very occasionally, we would get an intercept of a *"Flat Jack"*, the airborne search radar which was mounted in the rotodome of the *"Moss"* – the Tupolev Tu-126, or the *"Duga"* – an over-the-horizon radar.

I checked the lads' work and found that they were well on top of it.

Each week it was my job to collate all the information and make up a signal, which had to be typed up, and though that was not my job I found that I had to do it, because the sergeant whose appointed job it was could not type. He was a telephonist, who, on the consolidation of the trade groups, had been remustered on paper to a Teleg II.

A square peg in a round hole!

When I had become fully conversant with our side of the equation, I often took the chance to visit the ELINT intercept section to get the feel of how the operators worked and used their N/APR9 receivers.

It was, in effect, very similar to the work of the Morse, radio-teleprinter, and language operators.

The aerials they used were directional, and though most of the intercepts were in the centimetric X-band, with wavelengths of around three centimetres and frequencies from 8,500 to 10,680 Gigaherz, some were in Ku-band and L-band – mainly long-range surveillance radars like *Squat Eye* and *Flat Face.*

By definition, *"The observation, recording and technical processing for later intelligence purposes of information on foreign, non-communications, electromagnetic radiations emanating from other than atomic detonation sources"*, ELINT formed a perfect sister operation to SIGINT, whose definition was similar, if one deleted the rest of the sentence after 'foreign' and substituted 'communications' for 'non-communications'.

All work and no play is no good for any man, and I was always on the lookout for yet another string to my bow, and one soon came up.

One of my acquaintances, another Flight Sergeant, told me one day about a sailing course he had been on, and it sounded like a great opportunity.

The course was at Kiel, and it was entirely free.

My wife, a very understanding woman, who knew that a man had to do what a man had to do, agreed immediately.

'You must go.' She told me.

I sent off the application and received a letter back with a questionnaire to complete regarding my experience of yachts and navigation.

That was quickly filled in and despatched, and only a couple of days later I received the instructions for attending the course, most surprised to find that I would be doing the six-day course which could lead to the internationally accepted Coastal Skipper certification and not the five-day introductory course.

No sooner said than arranged, and a month later I flew to Kiel, the capital and most populous city of Schleswig-Holstein, its population around a quarter of a million. It is arguably the most important maritime centre in Germany, renowned for holding international sailing events, which include the biggest sailing event in the world – Kiel Week. It was also home to the sailing events of the 1936 Olympics and the 1972 Summer Olympics.

After I'd introduced myself to the instructors and the other four guys who would be sharing the twenty-five foot keelboat with me, we were shown to our very comfortable quarters and then given an excellent meal.

At seven o'clock the next morning we assembled at the boat, and for the first four hours were asked, one at a time, to demonstrate our familiarity with sea charts and navigation, the various ropes and parts of the rigging, the uses of sea-cocks and bilge pumps, and then as a group questioned on our knowledge of 'rules of the road' at sea, meteorology, tide tables, pilotage techniques, points of sail, emergency techniques, use of fenders, pontoons and warps and the correct response to a man overboard if we were skippering a craft.

From the multiple hands raised and quick answers it seemed that we had all done our homework before arriving at Kiel and were well up to speed, and the session was brought to a close in time for lunch.

After another great meal we cast off for an afternoon practice sail, and John, the ex-Pongo instructor, who, I found later, had the same sort of sense of the ridiculous that I had, gave each of us in turn an hour-long stretch as skipper, watching carefully how we rigged the boat as he gave repeated instructions to go about and jibe, run the yacht on every point of sail and on both tacks, from close hauled to a broad reach, finally having the skipper bring the yacht up into the wind.

We each made mistakes, due to lack of familiarity with the vessel, but none were so serious that they put the yacht in jeopardy, and by the end of the afternoon I could see that John was quite satisfied with our efforts.

The next day we spent sailing all day, with two hours each as skipper.

That day, very few mistakes were made, and at the end of it John told us we would be casting off on the morrow for a four-day voyage to Denmark and Sweden.

It was great.

Each one of us in turn was given the navigation to do to reach particular points on first of all the Danish coast, where we came across a strange phenomenon – brush buoys – weird-looking things that stood up out of the water like witches brooms, making one wonder if in that country, instead of burning the poor souls at the stake, they had drowned them, and the witches had shoved their brooms up into the air, hoping someone would pull them out again. They were very different from the port and starboard buoys we were used to, but just as efficient once one understood the system.

Then we sailed across to the Swedish coast before heading home.

For the first two days we were blessed with a steady, fifteen-knot, south-westerly breeze – easy sailing - but on the third, with a strong south-easter, gusting occasionally to near gale force, we had a real test of our ability to sail well. John watched each of us closely to see how we handled it and seemed satisfied. On the fourth day the wind dropped to almost nothing for a couple of hours around midday, but then picked up enough to see us home.

The navigation I found as easy as falling off a log. What happened in the air in ten minutes took half a day on the water – time to check every calculation a dozen times or more, if necessary.

Two of the others struggled a bit with it, and, of course, it was not something you could learn in ten minutes. I had had the benefit of two years, and stacks of practice.

We arrived back at Kiel well before tea time, and had a debriefing session first.

John congratulated all of us and then announced that two of us, Peter Collins, an Army sergeant stationed near Dortmund, and I had qualified as Coastal Skippers, and would be given certificates.

He told the others that they had only failed to reach the required standard because their navigation was not quite up to scratch and suggested they return for another shot at it after more practice at the art.

I flew back to Berlin well chuffed.

That certificate was to give me the chance, many years later, of becoming a full-time, salaried yacht skipper in the Greek Islands. It was another career turning point that I considered seriously, but did not take up.

I was back to the family, the rabbits and the Elint reporting, but I was still watching those deer – particularly the herd of five, and I knew their habits and their regular movements.

How to shoot a couple without being found out was an intriguing exercise, but the answer came that winter, on a day when it was twenty below and blowing a gale, with the snow coming sideways.

Thinking back, I must have been crazy; if I'd injured myself, or even become disorientated for half an hour, I would have surely frozen to death, but the old 'shit or bust' syndrome was back at work.

I drove to the edge of the runway, knowing that the control tower would not be manned, left the car there and walked off into the almost blinding snow.

They almost fooled me, I guess because the weather had made them change their habits.

As I neared the fence at the far side of the airfield, out of the gloom from my right and crossing my path there appeared a roe, hardly moving forward.

I lifted the shotgun and dropped it, then re-loaded that barrel in case I needed to use another shot.

Taking a pace forward to check that it was dead, and to start to take it back to the car, I was taken again by surprise when another one appeared.

That too went down.

And then three more walked into sight.

I shot a third.

Stupid man! I had to get them back to the car - if I left one out on the airfield I would be in dead trouble.

I only had one rope with me and had to tie it round three necks.

Luckily, despite the weight – around a hundred and sixty pounds - the bodies slid almost effortlessly over the snow, but lifting them into the trunk was not so easy.

You can imagine my wife's face when she came home from work and went into the bathroom for a wee when she came home from work, before I could warn her.

Those three deer were in the bath!

The ground was frozen solid, but I had long before prepared a trench, just in case I got lucky, and by the next afternoon the carcases and innards were well buried.

We had venison for the rest of our stay in Berlin.

While the snow was on the ground I had another little brush with it.

One of the duties I had was to take his supper out to the lad manning the D/F hut close to the camp outer fence, and for that purpose used the section Beetle.

Like all of the service VWs, it was functional, and that is about all you could say in its favour, but it was the pride and joy of our Flight Lieutenant, who treated it as if it was his personal baby.

I'd done the run dozens of times, and liked to get the little car up to top speed and skid round the perimeter track.

One frosty night I had delivered the supper and was driving back flat out, delighting in the slides that I had to keep correcting, using the perimeter track as my own private skid pan.

I crossed the runway, which had been cleared of snow, but as I reached the other side of it I completely lost control, when the vehicle hit a patch of black ice.

Immediately afterwards, sliding sideways at about seventy, the right hand front wheel hit one of the runway lights that were sunk into the ground, but had four-inch high glass domes fitted over them.

That side of the car lifted forty degrees into the air, and on two wheels the Volkswagen began to spin, and spin, and spin.

It must have gone round at least twenty-five times, hardly slowing at all on the sheet of ice.

The hangar loomed nearer and nearer.

At last the wheels came down onto the ground again, and I eased the car out of the spin and was able to dab the brakes momentarily.

When the car finally came to a halt, the hangar door was no more than ten yards away!

I made no report about the incident, of course, since it was my own stupid fault, and there was no visible damage, but shortly afterwards the Flight Lieutenant told me, 'I can't make it out, but my Volkswagen just isn't driving right. It seems to be crabbing. It *was* all right until last week.'

Keeping a straight face, I assured him, 'That is a sort of general fault with them, sir, when they've done a few miles. It's something to do with tyre wear.'

'Is it really?' He looked puzzled. 'Do you know, I never knew that.'

I hoped he would not discuss it with the MT officer!

I had been interested in 'ham' radio throughout my service career, and had done several stints on a friend's set-up at Digby, so as a result knew a lot of the 'ham' abbreviations, like '88', which meant 'love and kisses', '73' - 'best regards' and '14' – the weather.

I had not applied for a licence in the UK, since one had to sit a Post Office examination, and I couldn't be bothered, with everything else I was interested in, but in Germany, my experience as a wireless operator was accepted without further ado, and I applied for and obtained a licence.

The British forces in Germany were issued with callsigns beginning with 'DL2', and the callsign I was issued with was DL2XD. I was licensed to transmit with 50 watts of power and bought cheaply from a guy who was being repatriated a Johnson Viking Ranger transmitter and a Hallicrafters 120S receiver, plus all the gubbins that went with being a 'ham', then ordered from a printer in Berlin two hundred QSL cards, which one sent to anyone with whom one had made contact.

Of course, we in the 'Y' Service were not supposed to have contact with anyone in the Eastern Block or Russia, and after sending out a 'CQ' – a 'general call' - inviting any other 'ham' to answer, had to ignore any attempt by such an operator to contact us. Though I found plenty trying to call me I had been warned that most of them would be from the espionage networks, wanting contacts in the west. I felt there had been enough unwelcome interest in our doings, without wanting to attract the attentions of our Intelligence Services by working such contacts, and avoided them like the plague. In any case, there were plenty of other countries in the world whose operators were keen to 'work' me, and the walls of my little station were soon plastered with dozens of cards.

Fifty watts did not give one much scope, and being of my devious mind-set, I thought of a better arrangement.

When the station was not doing any flying, and the control tower was not manned, which meant most late evenings and nights, the station transmitters, a wartime-vintage Marconi T1509 and a SWB8 – usually called a SWAB8 by those in the trade – from the same manufacturer, were not switched on. The 1509 gave out 300 watts and the SWAB on full power 3.5 Kilowatts.

One late evening I crept into the transmitter room, switched on the 1509 and used it to send out a series of CQs, chuffed to be able to use Morse and RT to contact countries I'd never been able to reach before.

As a natural progression, it was not long before I used the SWAB too, as detuned as I could make it, and the contacts I made were fabulous.

Even detuned it must have been chucking out something like half a Kilowatt, and I knew using it was taking too much of a chance, so went back to the 1509.

Even with that there were some dodgy moments, like the time when a guy on the West Coast of America asked me how, with only fifty watts of power, I could have a five-by-nine signal reaching him and almost blowing his head off.

'What the hell kind of antenna have you got there, fella?' He asked.

With fingers firmly crossed, I told him jokingly, 'A thick piece of string with the end in a big puddle.'

It was obvious that if I persisted in using the two powerful transmitters I would eventually be caught out, and went back to my Viking Ranger for the rest of my tour, but changed the Hallicrafters. It was not up to the job, in my opinion.

Another thing I spent time on was piano lessons.

The Officers' Mess bought a new piano, and the old one was going begging.

With tremendous difficulty, we shoved and dragged it up the stairs into our quarter, and I started to learn to play.

I was never much good, but the practice came in very handy later in life, when I bought a series of organs and then keyboards, the last one of which makes me sound like a forty-piece orchestra, with pre-recorded authentic backing tracks by my favourite bands of the 40s and 50s – Glenn Miller and Benny Goodman, where all I have to do is play the lead instrument. 633 Squadron comes out great too.

Wanting to have a new car to take back with me without paying the swingeing purchase tax, I ordered one of the iconic Capris, a new Ford only introduced the previous year – the GT XLR model – absolutely top of the range, with every extra they could load on it.

Delivery time came up, and I had to fly home to collect it from the Export Showroom at 88 Regent Street, in London.

Standing in that showroom it looked fantastic. I'd ordered the flame red paintwork with a matt-black bonnet – a really macho combination.

It looked as if it was ready to take off to Mars, and I was inordinately proud of it before ever sitting on the driver's seat.

The agent opened the door and invited me to get in.

I needed no prompting.

After he'd shown me how everything worked, I started the engine and listed to its wonderful beat, blipping the throttle to hear that lovely sound.

It all seemed top notch until I asked him, 'Where is the spare set of keys?'

Smiling, he said, 'They'll be in the ashtray.'

I pulled it out.

It was full of dark red, furry stuff.

His smile disappeared, and his face flushed deep red, showing his intense embarrassment.

I asked, 'Is this rust?'

It was.

I fudged around in the mess and pulled out the spare set of keys, rusted to hell.

I flung myself out of the car and demanded, 'I want my money back! This bloody thing has been standing in a field for two years!'

He grovelled, apologising profusely.

I knew positively that he had had no idea of where the car had been, but I was on a loser.

He pointed out that the export laws were extremely strict. The car had been ordered off the export list, and had to be delivered to the person who had ordered it. There was no way that the deal could be altered.

On placing a firm order, the full price had to be paid, and I had done just that.

I was stuck with it.

I must say that driving it was a delight, but despite my efforts with Aquaseal there was no stopping the rust, and I sold it the week that the year was up after returning to the UK, trading it in for a new Cortina GT, which thankfully was not such a rust bucket.

It was not the only problem I had with new cars off the export list.

My wife fancied a Mini, and I bought her one.

That one I arranged to have delivered to the factors in Berlin, so that we could pick it up from the showroom there.

It duly arrived and seemed like a nice little car, if not my personal style.

Another thing about it was that it was so low to the ground that even up on ramps I could not crawl underneath to underseal it.

Jacquie enjoyed driving it, but when it had done only three thousand miles I noticed that the tyres looked as if they had done twenty thousand, the tread seriously worn down.

I complained at the showroom.

They looked and agreed with me that something was not right. They must have been a bad batch of tyres, they told me, and replaced the whole set, free of charge.

I kept watch, and after only one thousand miles there was serious wear again. Not only that, but the chrome strips were showing pitting and discoloration and the paint near the sills looked as if it was about to flake off.

I gave one of the mechanics in the MT section a few marks to put the Mini up on the hoist at the weekend so that I could look underneath.

My language during the two minutes that followed that look up at the underbody was enough to blister any paintwork!

There was a gash almost three feet long and more than two inches deep running diagonally across.

The Mini had been dropped from quite a distance, probably when it was being unloaded from the ship by crane, and had landed on something hard and sharp edged.

Back to the showroom I went, murder on my mind.

I made them put the car up on a hoist and inspect it.

Yes, they admitted, I was right.

I demanded a new car in place of that one.

Impossible, they told me. It was ordered off the export list and blah, blah, blah.

Oh, yes, I knew all about that, I told them and groaned.

I pointed out the chrome work. They would change it all, they said – no problem.

I pointed out the paintwork. We'll completely re-spray it for you, they said.

'What is my wife supposed to drive while you are doing that?' I asked.

'We'll supply a car', they said.

I left the Mini there and drove the loaned vehicle home.

Jacquie wanted to keep it; she liked the colour better.

I sat down, my pen almost on fire, and wrote a personal letter to Lord Nuffield, the chairman of the British Motor Company, demanding compensation.

A nice letter arrived almost by return, containing a lot of platitudes, but nothing concrete. The matter was being investigated, it said, and was signed by a facsimile of Lord Nuffield's signature.

Jacquie's Mini came back.

Every bit of chrome had been changed and it had been re-sprayed.

Whoever had wielded the spray gun must have learnt his trade on a Friday afternoon. The orange peel was dreadful.

I tried to polish it out, but after three hours I'd only done the bonnet.

Nevertheless, we held onto it and my wife continued to drive it.

Less than a month later the chrome started to pit again, and I noticed heavy wear on the tyres.

Back again to the showroom, fuming.

Another re-spray and another change of all the chrome.

Three days after we got it back, I advertised it on the notice board at Summit House and sold it cheaply to a soldier in one of the regiments stationed in the Divided City. He seemed delighted.

I had written three letters to Lord Nuffield, and finally received one with an apology, but worded in such a way that gave no hope for compensation.

I vowed that I would never again own a car made by the British Motor Company, but against my better judgement and after many days of attempted persuasion gave in to my wife's desire to own another Mini.

That was one of the best cars we ever owned, and she drove it for almost ten years without a single problem.

CHAPTER SEVENTEEN

The day I had worked for during the previous five years – more if one included the study for Latin and the 'A' level examinations – loomed ever closer, and I did a lot of last minute cramming.

Two days before the Finals, I flew back to London and the Union Jack Club again, making sure that I arrived in plenty of time, in case of flight problems.

I was shaking inside as I waited on the pavement with other students taking their Finals.

One thing really got up my nose: the Reading List for the examination had over fifty books on it. Without knowing any better, I had studied all of them. When I told the others around me they could not believe it.

They had all known for the last two years of their study *WHICH SIX BOOKS* would be the subject of the literature paper, and not only that, *WHICH PAGES of those books!*

I had done hundreds of hours of unnecessary study.

Of course, in retrospect, it made me a far better student, but I had not the depth of knowledge of those pages that they had.

Despite my worrying, I found the examinations easy, particularly the translations. Let's face it, I'd had enough experience of that facet of the syllabus.

I flew back to Germany sure that I had done enough for a Grade One.

It felt like a complete anticlimax, being back with no urgent study to do, and it seemed like a holiday, despite having to do my job.

I had time to spare and think up new things to do.

I got together some of the other lads who had expressed an interest in shooting on the camp and suggested we build a run and buy a hundred or so pheasants poults, so that we could have a couple of decent shoots when the season began.

We clubbed together, built the pen of chicken wire, strung around several trees, bought a hundred and twenty pheasant poults from a breeder and enough feed for them for the next few months.

They did well, and the day before we intended to shoot we let them out.

The next day we drove the wood they had been in, expecting terrific sport, but saw not one bird.

We covered the entire camp. Nothing!

Then we began searching and came upon some feathers and some newly turned over earth.

Buried beneath it we found a hundred and eighteen pheasants.

In one night a fox, or several foxes, had killed every one of them!

So much for our excursion into pheasant rearing.

One day, waiting for my daughter to fly in to Templehof on holiday from boarding school, I got into a conversation with the lady sitting next to me, a Spanish lady I thought.

The plane was delayed by three quarters of an hour, and the two of us chatted away about all sorts of things, with me pleased to be able to practice my Spanish with a native speaker.

At last the aircraft landed, and as we parted my companion made a little bow and said, 'Grazie, signor.'

Only then did I realise that she had been speaking Italian.

We had understood each other perfectly!

Of course, you can guess where we went on our next holiday later that month.

My wife vowed never to go back. In Milan her bottom was pinched very hard three times in the crowds. Sheron, too, had her bottom pinched, but said it didn't hurt.

There was one very amusing incident during our time in the country.

We were off the road in a small wood, having a makeshift picnic, when a young Italian drove up in an open-top, flame red sports job and parked next to my car. He jumped out and began haranguing me with two armfuls of watches.

I had to buy one, he insisted; they were all terrific value and top quality; stolen goods, he said, and therefore very cheap.

I was annoyed and told him to 'levati dalle palle' – (piss off), I already had a perfectly good watch – an Omega. I lifted my wrist and showed it to him.

He would not take no for an answer and persisted.

He'd interrupted my meal and I was not in the best of tempers.

I improved on the first bit of vernacular I'd used, having learnt the swearwords first in the language, as in most that I had studied, and told him to 'Vaffanculo'.

He began jumping up and down in rage, then leapt into his car, and with the engine screaming, shoved it into reverse.

The wheels spun, throwing up gouts of earth, and the car hurtled backwards, ran up a steep bank and stopped, with both back and front wheels in the air.

It rocked backwards and forwards a few times then came to rest, perfectly balanced.

He clambered out, frantic with rage, and kicked the bank several times, using other swearwords I hadn't learnt.

They sounded most impressive, and I made a mental note to add them to my active vocabulary.

The pantomime went on for several minutes before he realised that if he wanted to get the car down he would need my help with a tow rope.

He approached me and in fractured English asked for my assistance.

I told him in equally fractured Italian – or maybe it was Spitalian - that I intended carrying on with my lunch. I turned my back on him.

Several disgusting epithets later he realised that I had no intention of helping him, and he took to the road, stomping off on foot to fetch help.

We finished our picnic and left.

My wife did tell me I was a heartless bugger, but was smiling when she said it.

All British Forces and other personnel stationed in Berlin who had a quarter were entitled to a maid.

Ours during the first tour had been a sour-faced, but highly efficient sixty-five year old, who annoyed me greatly at times by trying to give us advice on how to bring up our daughter; usually ridiculous advice.

One blazing hot summer's day, when it was almost ninety degrees in the shade, we had taken Sheron, who was six months old at the time, for a walk in the pram.

When we returned, our maid ran downstairs to greet us.

She took one look in the pram and almost screamed, 'Ach! Keine Mütze!' – no hat.

I screamed too, 'Gerda! Um Gottes willen!'

Did she want the baby to die of heat exhaustion?

Of course, a German woman would have the baby wearing a hat, regardless, and she was only respecting tradition.

Her intentions were good.

On the present tour, we had as our maid a plumpish but attractive forty-three year old, Renate, who had the blackest hair I have ever seen on a white person.

She, too, was highly efficient, and we were well satisfied with her.

With Jacquie working four days a week at Summit House, Renate's services were highly appreciated.

She had been working for us for just over a year when we returned from a holiday in Austria to find her sitting at the dining room table, dressed in black and sobbing.

The previous afternoon, she had returned home after work to find her twelve-year old son, Heinz, in the garden, trying desperately to hold his father's body higher, to release the pressure on his neck from the rope with which he had hanged himself from a tree. The boy had found him far too late.

I took her home in the car and told her not to come back to work until she was ready to.

A week later she came to see me, breaking down in tears when she told me that Heinz was suffering from terrible trauma, and was off school. She would have to stay home to look after him.

It was a blow, and we needed a maid, so I placed advertisements in two of the Berlin newspapers.

So many maids were needed that it was difficult to find one, but after a week without a reply I received one from a woman who sounded ideal.

We arranged an interview and I drove down to the guardroom at the appointed time to find a vision of loveliness waiting for me.

Three pairs of lecherous eyes were gazing out of the guardroom window, entranced, and I could clearly see why.

She was around thirty, with a figure that would have graced any catwalk and an eye-catching bust, and was clad in a beautifully tailored, lilac, shantung dress that screamed 'designer', its lower half in ruffles that began small and increased in size down to the hem, just two inches above her knees. A tiny dove-grey waistcoat completed the ensemble.

Her make-up looked professionally done, and her corn-blonde hair was piled up on her head in a highly attractive bouffant style. To cap it all, almost unbelievably, she had in her left hand a minute, elegant handbag, and in her right hand the tiniest lace-edged parasol.

I almost looked for the ubiquitous white poodle.

This could not be the woman who had applied for the position of maid, could it? She looked as if she had just stepped out of a millionaire's front door.

Side benefits loomed large in my thoughts.

I could not possibly be so lucky.

She introduced herself and I held the passenger door open for her.

She slid onto the seat demurely and drew her legs in without the slightest sign of an inch of thigh, an act that had to be learnt to be so perfect.

I drove her to the quarter, offered her a drink, which she declined, and began questioning her.

Her voice matched the rest of her – low and well modulated – sexy, in fact, or was I hopefully imagining it?

She needed the job, she told me, because she had recently divorced her husband due to his adultery, and now had no income.

I was sure that she had never done a day's housework in her life, but she assured me that she had and could do the job efficiently.

I had to give her a trial, didn't I? Oh, come on! Be reasonable – I *had* to.

She said she could start immediately – right away, in fact, and I shrugged and agreed. She certainly wasn't dressed for it, but perhaps she intended divesting herself of her dress. One could only hope.

As she rose from her chair she winced and uttered, 'Aah', clutching her lower stomach.

I was instantly concerned and asked her if the pain came often.

Several times a day, she said, and was getting worse.

I asked her to show me exactly where the pain was, and she laid her hand on a place which told me almost certainly what ailed her.

I asked (for medical reasons only – you have to believe me) if I could touch her stomach.

She nodded, and I asked her if she would lie down on the bed. (All right – I admit it – I had nefarious intent).

I led her through to the bedroom and helped her to lie down.

With just two fingers I tried to feel my way through the layers of dress material to touch McBurney's Point.

It was impossible – there was just too much material in the way.

I tut-tutted, and she suggested, 'Would it be easier if I lifted the dress?'

Was she putting it all on, and was this a seduction scene?

I had to wonder, although I knew from past experience that the Germans, like most Europeans, have a much more robust attitude to the naked body and its functions than the English.

With heart thumping so loudly I thought she must be able to hear it, I agreed, and she pulled the hem up to waist level.

It did not surprise me that she was wearing black lace panties, which, though not totally transparent, had enough half-inch holes in the lace to make imagination completely unnecessary.

She pulled the top of the panties down a couple of inches.

I lifted my head, looking away, but not before I'd had a good glimpse, naturally, and touched her bare belly, my fingers feeling as if they were on fire, and another part of my body reacting violently.

She gasped loudly, and I knew the answer. She was not play acting.

I told her, 'Sie haben eine sehr gefährliche Blindarmentzündung'.

Her appendix was in a dangerous state, and could burst at any time, killing her. Peritonitis was not something to be disregarded.

After another stolen look at the forbidden fruits, I told her to pull her dress down; I would call for an ambulance.

She began to cry, and I asked, 'Have you no insurance?'

She shook her head.

I felt desperately sorry for her, but there was nothing I could do.

I was feeling sorry for myself too. I had been offered a glimpse of Heaven, and it had been snatched away from me.

Ah, well, maybe it was for the best. I've always been a fatalist and know that all these things are planned Up There.

A couple of weeks later, Renate came back to work for us.

CHAPTER EIGHTEEN

Though I was sure that I had done well in the Finals, I was on tenterhooks until I received the official result.

I had done well, but not as well as I had hoped: I had achieved a Batchelor of Arts Degree, Second Class.

Either a One or a Two is classed as a 'Good Honours Degree', so I knew I should be happy with it.

I ordered a mortar-board and gown to wear at the Degree Ceremony, knowing that I would probably need it in any teaching job I landed.

After receiving my degree from Doctor Landers' hands, he asked me to see him after the ceremony finished.

I didn't need to say anything; he gave me a knowing look and said, 'I know you expected a One and that you are disappointed, but let me tell you two things: first of all, the degree you have is a fine one – one that you fully deserved and should be extremely proud to have achieved, and secondly, the University never gives a One to an external student.'

He held his hand up as I began to protest.

'For one reason only: other universities would insist that it meant our degree examinations are too easy. It is a great shame for people like you.'

I told him I would shortly be looking for a teaching post, and he insisted that I give his name and address to any school I applied to, so that he could send them a reference.

I thanked him sincerely for that and for all his help.

After Christmas that year I began taking the *Times Educational Supplement*, looking to see what teaching jobs were being advertised, and what kind of qualifications were needed for them.

I'd considered other occupations, but decided to go for teaching as a job with equivalent pay to that which I was then receiving, and which had the same six weeks or more of holiday.

I wanted to go back to my roots and get a job in Norfolk.

There were a few advertised that might suit me, but it was too early to apply for the summer term.

From the beginning of February, adverts for the next term started to appear, and I found two that I liked the look of.

One was at The Norwich School, the top private school in my home city – a one-year post, or so it was advertised, but I knew that was often done so that the new incumbent could be got rid of without fuss if he or she had not come up to scratch.

The other was at Costessey High School, in the village in which I grew up.

That was for a post teaching half English/half PE for one term, after which the intention was to introduce a language, preferably German, into the school syllabus. It sounded ideal for me.

I applied for both posts, and about a week later received replies, inviting me to attend for interview. The date of the Costessey interview was given, the other job was for 'a date to be arranged'.

I flew home from Berlin, hired an MGB GT from the Hertz desk at Gatwick, and drove to Norwich, where I telephoned both Headmasters.

The Head of the Norwich School greeted me warmly over the phone and said he would be delighted to see me that day at my convenience but added, 'You realise, of course, that the post advertised is a temporary one for only one year?'

I told him I did, and he astonished me with, 'You see, from the letters of recommendation I have received from Professor Yuile and Doctor Landers it seems that you are far too highly qualified for such a lowly post. I am sure that you deserve better.'

I was stunned. My little bit of grammar learning must have made one hell of an impression on the two learned men.

I thanked him for his comments and told him that I had another interview with a State school that day and if offered that post I would take it, but if it fell through I would like to be considered for the job at the Norwich School.

He accepted that and reiterated that he would be pleased to interview me if I wished. I had two strings to my bow.

To be fully accredited as a teacher, one also had to have a degree in Teaching. If employed in a private school, the only way to achieve that would be to take two years off to attend university and sit the examinations.

If employed in a State school, the two years' experience counted as the required time element, and one could sit for the Diploma in Education at the end of it.

The Headmaster at Costessey High School, Mr Reeve, was less ebullient when I spoke to him, and his tone made me wonder if I had already been rejected as a possible candidate in his mind, but he told me what time to report for interview.

Had I known that one of the six candidates being interviewed was the Deputy Headmaster's son-in-law, I would not have bothered to turn up, but turn up I did, and was shown into a waiting room where the five others who had attended for interview sat upright on hard chairs in a row, giving me the impression of five targets on a fairground shooting stall, which in the light of the events that followed was a fair analogy.

First, we were interviewed one after another by the Head, Deputy Head and Senior Master. I had the clear impression when I was in with them that they were merely going through the motions and were not interested, although they were polite enough.

I was told again what I had learnt from the advertisement - that the intention was to introduce a foreign language to the school after the autumn holidays, and that the appointed candidate would be expected to form a department for that purpose. If that introduction was successful, a second language would be added after another one or two years.

The guy who I learnt later was the son-in-law was in there for less than ten minutes, but the rest of us were grilled for almost half an hour each.

It should have told us something.

After those interviews came a second lot with the School Governors.

I got on well with them – they were my kind of people, good old Norfolk boys, every one of them, and they made it clear that their most important requirement was someone who could use discipline to control unruly classes. My background in the RAF seemed to inspire them with confidence.

At the end of my interview the Chairman smiled and told me I had the job.

After I had been teaching for about five years I was speaking to one of them on Sports Day, out on the playing field, and he told me that what had impressed the Board of Governors most was the fact that my shoes had such a beautiful shine.

All that Air Force bullshit had finally paid off!

I walked back out of the interview room, closed the door and grinning widely I shook my hands over my head, fingers locked in a victory gesture, and told them with glee that they could go home. It was wicked of me, but typical of my unregulated sense of humour.

Their expressions and reactions would have looked grand on film.

The son-in-law looked stunned, though at the time I did not know why.

A year later the Deputy Head admitted to me that I had not been their choice of candidate at the time, but that he was now glad I had been selected.

I flew back to Berlin as if on a cloud.

Maybe it was that euphoria which led to me committing what was looked on as a cardinal sin in my job.

I had always believed that the way the intercept stations were laid out could be much improved. The linguist set rooms were separate from the Morse/Radioteleprinter intercept rooms, and when the Russians indicated switching to voice or vice versa, it meant a telephone call to the other set room and a frantic searching for the frequency on the part of the other operator.

I had three times on various stations suggested that for those Russian and East German nets that regularly changed from one method of transmission to the other, it would be infinitely more efficient to have the voice operator sitting at his receiver next to the Morse guy. He could then merely shove his earphone jack plug into the other man's set when the enemy station changed to voice transmission and immediately start logging.

It had all fallen on deaf ears.

That was the reason I had taught myself Russian, and I had for the last several years always logged the voice on the same page I was using for Morse when they 'went over'.

Among the radars whose times of transmission we were collating, there appeared locally a SAM engagement radar new to our area, the *9S32M, NATO designaton "Grill Pan"*, along with its associated acquisition radar, which had the NATO designation *"Bill Board" – the 9S15M*. It was determined that those radars were used with the Russian SAM-23 surface-to-air missile system, and they were being intercepted from around the Oranienburg airfield, only 35 kilometers from Berlin, which meant that the Soviet's latest SAM system had been introduced into East Germany.

They were known radars, having been intercepted for some time around the Black Sea area by the Yanks, but the intercepts had been long-range, with no knowledge of their efficiency.

There had been several messages sent by us to our Transatlantic cousins, and by them to us concerning those radars, and the need to obtain their parameters, but no one seemed to be doing much about it.

I made a suggestion to the three officers who reported on our findings that voice, Morse, radar and D/F results could be tied together to obtain those parameters, but it was ignored. Not possible, they said.

We kept logging hours of "*Bill Board*" activity, and another with the designation "*High Screen*", the 9S19M, which was also connected with the SAM-23 – Russian designation "*Antey2500*"

I went to look at the Morse and voice intercepts taken at the time when the Migs were doing their calibration runs with the new system, and there were gaps where the ground operator changed from Morse to voice as the aircraft began their runs. Gaps that made it impossible to be accurate in plotting.

One Saturday, my day off, I went in and sat at a spare receiver, tuned in to the Oranienburg ground controller's frequency and sat waiting until the day's exercise began. When it did, I logged Morse and voice until the exercise finished, with timing down to the second logged against each transmission.

The next day, the Sunday, I obtained the American and British radar intercepts of the aircraft runs, which gave me their headings and speeds. I then married those up with the voice and Morse intercept, second by second, and plotted every run on a three-hundred and sixty degree chart.

It clearly showed the acquisition capabilities of the SAM and the distances from the aircraft at which the spoof missile shots were reportedly made.

It was obvious that the maximum working range was approximately seventy-five kilometres.

It took less than two hours to write a report, with the chart to back it up, and the next morning I presented it to my bosses.

The shit hit the fan.

Who the hell was I, a mere reporting analyst, to suggest that I was capable of writing a report?

They pooh-poohed it and were going to ignore it.

I was wild, and, I suppose stupidly, went over their heads to the Squadron Leader.

He read the report and told me he thought it was excellent, but gave me a rocket for being so presumptuous. The way he said it made me realise that what he really meant was that I had upset my superiors and should not have done so.

He made them publish it.

The Americans raved about it, with comments like, *"One of the best reports we have ever seen on a SAM system"*, which made matters worse.

Obviously, to continue the working relationship was impossible.

I was told to pack my bags and to go back to my old job in charge of the set room for the rest of my time in the Mob.

I had only two months left to serve and I didn't care. The acceptance of the report had exonerated me.

I soon fell back into the routine.

The operators, some of whom had been there as long as I had, expected me to become 'the old slave driver' again, but I was past caring if they slept on night duty.

That routine was broken suddenly in what was for me a delightful way.

We all knew about BRIXMIS – the British Military Mission, and its Soviet counterpart, SOXMIS. There were reciprocal agreements in force which allowed the former to drive around in East Germany and the latter to do the same in West Germany.

I'd spoken to a pongo staff sergeant who told me he drove one of the cars, and said it was exhilarating.

I was getting to the *'days to do – very few'* stage when I was asked to go and see the adjutant.

Wondering what I'd done wrong this time and not much caring I reported to his office.

He didn't waste time, 'You've been a rally driver; is that right, Nash?'

I told him it was.

'Are you willing to do a fast driving job?'

Again, I answered in the affirmative. It would be a change from the set room.

'Brixmis has a mission on, and their driver has had to go to hospital. They've asked for someone with your sort of experience. It means crossing into East Germany, but it will be perfectly legal, and you should be safe enough. Are you game?'

Could a fish swim?

I nodded enthusiastically, 'Certainly, sir.'

'Right!' he said, 'You need to leave immediately. Do you require transport?'

I said I would be happy to use my own car, and he told me where to report at the Berlin Stadium: to Brixmis, not to HQ Berlin Infantry Brigade.

'Off you go then. They are waiting for you.'

## CHAPTER NINETEEN

I'd been to the Stadium before, when I went to see the barrister, but was directed by the guardroom to Brixmis.

An anxious looking young Rupert with captain's pips on his shoulders was standing by a khaki-painted Ford Cortina, the new Mark III model, with full nomenclature printed in white lettering on the rear. The paintwork on the sides was badly scuffed, and I imagined the scuffing to be contrived to make the vehicle look sub-standard. I was wrong.

The adj. had telephoned to say that I was on my way, and the officer was expecting me.

He shook hands, 'Nice of you to volunteer, Nash. They tell me you can drive.' He had one eyebrow raised in query, and I told him he would be satisfied.

'Okay on forest tracks?'

'I've been on a few.' I smiled to myself, thinking of Betws y Coed, a couple of National forests, and an extremely hairy rally I had done in Norway.

'Good. Get in. We are late. Let's hope this weather doesn't deteriorate any more.'

The day had started sunny, but it had clouded over, and I fancied I could feel a spit of rain in the air.

I started the engine and heard a wonderful low burbling.

He was watching my face. 'Nice, isn't it?'

I nodded, grinning, knowing I was in for a great ride, 'What is it, sir, Lotus?'

'No, special Cosworth conversion. Top speed well over the ton. You can imagine the rest. And for the duration of this mission the name is Ted.'

I nodded, 'Tony.'

'Off we go then, Tony. Checkpoint Charlie to start with.'

To my surprise we were not stopped, but waved through by the Russians manning the checkpoint.

Immediately, three Vopo vehicles pulled out from the kerb, one by one, playing 'follow my leader' with us.

Ted grinned, flicking his head towards the rear, 'Those are what you have to lose, but not yet for awhile.'

He began to give me directions through East Berlin, and I noticed from the position of the sun that we were heading more or less east.

The Vopos stayed close behind.

As we left the city limits Ted reached over and grabbed a map case from the back seat.

He opened it and took out what looked to me like a detailed English Ordnance Survey map, but I knew it could not be one.

He saw my interest and told me, 'Special production, just for this job. One to ten thousand; six inches to the mile.'

I nodded my appreciation, 'Nice one.'

'Stick to about thirty miles an hour; they get nicely pissed off when we do that.'

'Roger.'

The road we were on was large enough to be a main one, but the surface was in a terrible condition, cracked, and with damned great potholes every few yards.

Not only had the car's engine been converted, but also its suspension, which was one of the hardest I had ever experienced.

We were 'doing a Bond', and like him we were shaken but not stirred.

The habitations became sparse; just the odd dilapidated farmhouse, and we entered long stretches of woods.

To begin with, they were made up of low, stunted pines, but it was not long before we entered thicker woods, containing taller pines, intermingled with deciduous trees.

Ted had been quiet apart from giving directions at crossroads and junctions, and I reckoned we had travelled about twenty miles from town when, coming up to a sharp bend he urged, 'Foot down now, Tony, flat out, and from now on obey my instructions instantly.'

We flew round the bend, the engine responding like a thoroughbred racehorse, and exited it doing over seventy.

There was another sharp bend a hundred yards on and we did a four-wheel slide around it on the soft blown sand that covered it, but came out of the slide quickly, now doing eighty-five.

'Right, Tony, now let's see what you are made of. In a second or two I am going to tell you to turn right. You'll need to brake like hell to do it, and I'll tell you when to start braking....brake now!'

I slammed on the anchors and the nose went down as if the front would hit the road.

'Turn....now!'

I did as ordered and found a wall of forest in front of me.

It looked as if he had deliberately forced us to crash.

I admit I closed my eyes, waiting for the crunch, but instead heard a brushing sound on both sides and underneath.

I opened my eyes and found that we were on an old, overgrown, narrow path. It had been invisible from the road; the branches of the trees had grown over it.

His explosive expulsion of breath told me that he had been holding it, as I had.

'Okay,' he murmured, 'you can take it as easy as you like now. We need to go about half a mile and then turn onto another track that leads to the airfield.'

'Oranienburg?'

He nodded, 'You've got it. Well done.'

We did three more changes of path, and then he told me, 'Very slow now. We need to stop in about fifty yards.'

When I'd brought the vehicle to a halt, I could hear the sound of jets nearby.

He opened his door and offered, 'You can have a kip if you like, or come and watch with me.'

I pushed open my door.

'I wouldn't miss any of this for the world.'

He grinned, 'Good man.'

He had taken a clipboard and a pair of large binoculars from beneath his seat, and I followed him to the edge of the wood.

From the tree line we watched one aircraft after another take off, fly out and disappear and then, a few minutes later, return and either land or disappear on a different heading.

Ted was recording everything: times, type of aircraft, headings, aircraft markings and rough heights.

It went on for about twenty minutes and then suddenly stopped.

All the aircraft that had been flying came in to land and did not take off again.

Ted nodded, 'Always happens. The bastards know we are somewhere in the vicinity, watching, and tell their air force to desist with whatever they've been doing, so that they give nothing more away. We can't do any more here, but there is one more port of call.'

'You were taking details of their spoof SAM runs, weren't you?'

Ted looked at me strangely, almost suspiciously.

'And just how do you know that?'

'I've been working on the ELINT and SIGINT side of that.'

His face cleared, 'I see I brought the right man with me today. Come on, wind that motor up again.'

He gave me directions along more forest tracks until we came to a clearing with a small farmhouse sitting on the far side of it.

The occupant must have heard us arrive, because he exited from the house and came over to the car as we stopped, looking worriedly all around him, as if he expected dozens of weapon-toting Vopos to suddenly leap out of the trees to arrest him.

He was a man of at least sixty, stooped and badly dressed, his craggy round face burnt dark brown by the sun, and favouring his right leg.

Ted got out, greeted him warmly and shook hands before handing over a heavy canvas bag.

The old man thanked him and in return gave him a sheet of paper.

Ted glanced at it and also gave his thanks.

I was scrutinised by a pair of suspicious eyes, 'You have a different driver. Can he be trusted?'

I didn't blame him in the least for being wary. I did not like to think of the treatment he would receive in the cellars of House Number One of the Stasi headquarters in the Lichtenberg district of Berlin if arrested by the Vopos for spying.

I told him in German, 'Don't worry, old friend, I am leaving Germany for ever in a couple of weeks and I am deaf and blind. You are completely safe.'

Ted glanced at me appreciatively.

He took his goodbyes, slapping the old man on the back.

As we drove off Ted asked where I'd learnt German and I told him part of my history.

'And you're leaving shortly?'

'Demob.'

'What a shame. You'd have been a good man to add to the team.'

'That makes me sad.' I told him, quite seriously, 'This is my kind of buzz.'

He directed me along paths that became wider and wider, although still grass covered, and then said, 'Road coming up in two hundred yards. Turn left when you reach it. Somewhere along that stretch we'll pick up our tail again.'

He was right. One of the Vopo cars was parked at the side of the road about two miles on and it pulled out and fell in behind us.

'Shall I stick to thirty again?' I asked.

Another grin, 'No, accelerate to seventy, then brake hard to twenty, then up to seventy again. You get the picture. Once we hit the town limits keep to thirty.'

The first time I braked we very nearly had a boot full of Vopos, but the driver learnt his lesson and kept back for the rest of the way.

By the time we drove past the first houses on the outskirts, one of the other Vopo cars had joined the first.

Again there was no stop at Checkpoint Charlie, though as I glanced at the faces of the Russians we passed it seemed to me that they were bloody angry and looked as if they would have liked to shake their fists at us, or possibly send a couple of bursts from their Nikonov assault rifles into the car.

Back at the Stadium, as we were saying our farewells and shaking hands I asked him how long he had been doing the job.

'Three years; about twice a week.'

I sighed, 'You're a lucky bugger, Ted.'

He nodded, 'Yes, I know I am, Tony.'

There are many sides to the Intelligence Community – many so-called 'INTS', some very modern and highly sophisticated, like some of the MASINTs – Measurement and Signature Intelligence – which includes laser, spectroscopic, and the IMINT part of that: Imagery Intelligence from satellites; GEOINT – Geospatial Intelligence from satellites; CYBINT/DNINT – Cyber and Digital Network Intelligence; TECHINT, and FININT – Financial Intelligence, alongside the comparatively low-level, but just as important HUMINT – intelligence from human sources, and SIGINT, which includes COMMINT –

Communications Intelligence, ELINT – Electronic Intelligence, and what is now called FISINT, previously known as TELINT – the collection and analysis of telemetry data.

Facing us, not only the Russians, but also the East Germans were doing the same thing to us, and in spades.

The East German intelligence service, run by the Stasi – the Ministerium für Staatssicherheit, was heavily into the Sigint business, as well as the Humint side.

HA III, their Sigint operation, controlled around ninety intercept stations in the Eastern Zone, with upwards of three thousand employees, who listened in to not only the radio communications of West Germany, but all radio and satellite-based telephone calls, faxes, data transmissions and Telexes.

It was big business, both sides of the wire.

I felt honoured that I had been able to give twenty years of my life to the three sides of SIGINT and was chuffed as little pigtails to have been able, in the last dying moments of my service, to add HUMINT to that collection, courtesy of that ancient East German farmer.

## CHAPTER TWENTY

As a send-off, a month before I left Gatow for the last time, they just had to do one more 'Exercise Rocking Horse'.

I went to my post, yawning, half wishing that the bloody Russians would come across, but, of course, they did not.

It was with ambivalent feelings that I took leave of my friends and departed from a life that I had enjoyed for almost a quarter of a century.

One door was closing, and another was opening.

I had four weeks' demob leave and two weeks' accumulated annual leave, and spent the beginning of it looking for a house.

I found one that I liked, which had two and a half acres of garden with it, only a quarter of a mile from the school.

It had been on the market at £9,750 for over eighteen months.

Foolishly, I offered the asking price.

The next day I was told someone had gazumped me.

I likely story! After eighteen months?

Anyway, that went on for some time until I told the agent it was my last word and offered £11,250.

Surprise, surprise! The offer was accepted.

With that out of the way, I began my new job, wearing, as they did at that time, my new gown and mortar board, feeling like a real professional.

I started teaching while I still had three weeks of service remaining in the Royal Air Force.

Though I knew the half time teaching PE would be highly enjoyable, out in the fresh air most of the time, it would not be demanding, and I was looking forward to the challenge of teaching English during the other half. It sounded reasonable enough, but what I did not know was that they had given me the 'sink class', 5X, the *Easter leavers*, to teach for two hours every day.

Very quickly they made me feel that I should have taken the job at the Norwich School.

It was the year that the School Leaving Age had been changed from 15 to 16, and the less able pupils who were affected did not like it one little bit. They were determined to make life as difficult as possible for the teachers who had to put up with them for the last three months of the school year.

Included in my class were eight girls and boys from the Home for Wayward Children, which was close behind the school playing field, and they included an arsonist, who was to set fire to the school twice the following year, a kleptomaniac, responsible for many thefts from the premises, and an angelic looking, curly-headed, blond haired, blue eyed boy, no more than four feet ten tall, who had stabbed his mother, a teacher and a social worker. Also in that class were four didicoy children and a 'Lolita' who regularly offered me every kind of sex out loud during class, causing huge merriment and bawdy comments from the others and great embarrassment to me. She insisted that she liked doing it with older men, would do *'anything'* and was really good at it.

I had no doubt she was right, and made certain that I was out in the corridor before the class every time, so that she could never be alone with me, after she had deliberately rubbed against me as she went past on the first day.

Strangely enough, she later became a kind of distant relative, and I received many reports of her lifestyle and the older men she had affairs with, followed by pregnancies, during the following years. She was a holy terror, and now, though in her late fifties, she is still happily playing the field.

It was impossible to teach those kids anything. They knew it all, they insisted, although some of them were almost illiterate. The worst part about it was that they did not care.

Discipline was virtually impossible, and I could not count the number of times the Headmaster suddenly appeared in my doorway, at which time the little so-and-sos would go completely silent, making me feel about two inches tall from embarrassment. He was nicknamed 'Spot' for his practice of creeping round the school on his crepe rubber soles, listening for any class where there was any unruly noise and throwing the door open when he heard it, with a demand, 'What is going on, Mr/Miss...?'.

He also spent most lunchtimes lying on the flat roof with a pair of binoculars, watching what the kids in the woods were up to. Mmm!

During the years since I left teaching, I have often come across quite a number of those

5X pupils in town and they always treat me deferentially and call me 'Sir'. It says something for our relationship, despite what it seemed like at the time.

During those three months that I taught them they deliberately created a living hell on earth for me, and every day of that period had me on the very point of walking out and leaving teaching forever.

But for the advice of a very experienced old teacher, I would have done just that.

His advice: 'Treat each lesson as a single unit. Just determine that whatever happens during that lesson, Tony, no matter how bad it is, you will last out to the end of it, and if you manage it, see it as a victory. Believe me, you are not alone. We are all in the same boat and we all feel as you do. Some of the staff who have been teaching for years regularly go into the loos for a good cry'.

His advice, and keeping the old RAF saying, '*Nilli illegitemi carborundum*' well in mind, were the only things that kept me going for most of the time, but there were still days when I had my hand on the doorknob, my running shoes on.

One of the very worst of those days was the last day of my RAF service, the 2nd of May, the day before my fortieth birthday, when the pupils seemed to realise that it was 'crunch' time, and played up so much that by three o'clock, worn to a frazzle, I had definitely decided to jack it in and find another job.

But I stayed, and that, as they say, is a whole different story.

If you have enjoyed this book, do please read some of my novels, and I would greatly appreciate it if you could leave a review. Thank you in anticipation.

25451461R00169

Printed in Great Britain
by Amazon